BACKYARD FARMING

TERRY BRIDGE

CHARTWELL
BOOKS, INC.

CONTENTS

INTRODUCTION

This is not a book about self-sufficiency, where no outside help is required to satisfy each individual's basic needs, especially with regards to the production of food. Instead, this is a guide to using to the optimum what available land you have, however small it may be, on which to grow a few vegetables and fruit for the family, or even to keep a few animals, provided the plot is large enough to support them. Even a city window box can be utilized, and a few large flower pots may be all you have to provide a little fresh produce for the table.

A backyard farm, which equates roughly with a smallholding or small farm, is one that is maintained without expectation of earning income from it. Or it may be intended to provide a sideline income, or be run as part of a lifestyle choice by people with the means to do so. However, it may simply be regarded as recreational land to be enjoyed by the entire family, and a

place where a few horses for the children may be kept and ridden.

A house with a large garden can be converted into a small hobby farm, with vegetables, poultry, rabbits and a few hives of bees, while an acre of land will support a couple of goats or pigs. Those with about 2.5 acres (10000m^2) at their disposal can begin to think about having poultry ranging free in an orchard, for example, or even about keeping a small flock of sheep. Double this area and a cow and a calf could be kept, while doubling it again to 10 acres (40000m^2), for example, would provide space enough to grow hay and forage crops in support of your livestock, or to establish an orchard planted with apples, plums and other fruit trees.

Even though they may be farming for the pleasure of it, with no expectations of any monetary gain,

OPPOSITE: Provided the soil is moderately fertile and the aspect not too shady, any patch of ground, however small, may be used to grow a few vegetables.

RIGHT: Rather more land, however, is needed to support a cow or two.

BACKYARD FARMING

OPPOSITE & BELOW: In the USA and elsewhere, many small farms have been swallowed up by larger concerns, freeing many of the farm buildings, with small plots of land attached, available for purchase.

many claim there is great satisfaction in making the land productive enough to cover the cost of feeding their livestock and supplementing the family menu with some organically-grown, high-quality food.

Today, as commercial farms continue to grow in size, in a quest to be economically viable, the land of smaller, more traditionally-run farms are swallowed up, although there may be little use for the buildings belonging

to them. These can be sold off with only a building lot of land, but are much more saleable if a modest 5 to 15 acres (20000 to 60000m²) comes along with them. Usually, these are snapped up by people with well-paid city jobs with a hankering for country life, by retirees wishing to keep active as part-time farmers, or for use as truck farms. Truck farming is the cultivation of one or a few fruit or vegetable crops on a

LEFT: Keeping chickens is a rewarding pastime, if only for the fresh eggs produced.

ABOVE: A few beehives will provide honey and also ensure that bee populations are maintained.

relatively large scale for transport to distant markets, where the crops cannot be grown, and which supplies produce for its own stands or regular stalls in local farmers' markets.

CHAPTER ONE
MAKING A START

Growing one's own vegetables is increasing in popularity. Not only is it an interesting and rewarding occupation, but crops are also fresher, better-tasting, and the vitamins and other benefits contained within them have more chance of being preserved.

Given the current concerns surrounding climate change, any reduction in journeys taken by our food to our tables will serve to reduce any adverse effects on the environment. It has been estimated that the ingredients making up the average festive family meal, could well clock up as many as 48,000 miles (77000km) or twice the circumference of the Earth. These 'food miles' all contribute to our carbon footprints, being the measure of the impact our activities have on the environment, so as well as cutting down

RIGHT & OPPOSITE: Growing our own food is not only beneficial to us as consumers but also helps preserve the environment.

OPPOSITE: Pot marigolds, grown among vegetables, repel aphids and other insects that routinely attack vegetable plants.

ABOVE: This potager, constructed like a formal parterre in the grounds of a French château, demonstates that vegetables can be just as attractive in this situation as the more usual flowers and ornamental plants.

on the energy we use, growing vegetables for our own use is another way of doing our bit in the fight against global warming.

The cut flower market clocks up even greater mileages, which can be offset by growing some cutting flowers yourself, for example, in an area being left fallow as part of a crop-rotation cycle. Alternatively, sow a few flower

seeds around and between vegetables, which will attract beneficial insects and in some cases repel pests, or use large flower pots scattered here and there.

A potager is a neat and ornamental way to grow vegetables for the pot, in which a series of beds are laid out in a formal pattern, with stones or low box hedges containing them, and the vegetables planted within these

boundaries. Here, some of the more colourful vegetables and herbs may also be grown, such as bright red- or yellow-stemmed chard, purple-podded peas, or rosemary, lavender and thyme.

Not all ground is suitable for growing food, and it is important to consider any previous activity which may have left a residue of contaminants. If the area has been used for burning rubbish, for example, there could well be dioxins present, which are the products of plastics combustion, and there may also be unsafe levels of heavy metals from paints and some printed materials.

To grow well, vegetables need to be suited to the local climate. They need an open position away from buildings and overhanging trees. The aspect of the site has a bearing on growth rates, therefore the ideal spot would be flat and south-facing, although a gentle slope would be less likely to be affected by spring frosts, in that cold air flows downhill. Sloping sites, on the other hand, are rather more difficult to use, in which case the plot may be set across

it. South-facing plots may need added watering in the hotter months to ensure the soil does not dry out.

Full sunlight is required for much of the day, but with shelter from strong winds. The best windbreaks should have 50 per cent permeability to allow some of the wind to pass through. Plant hedging around large plots or use netting around smaller one. When positioning your vegetables, place those that will grow taller where they will not cast shadows over the smaller ones. Try to plant sun-loving vegetables in south-facing positions and those that prefer shade facing north.

PREPARING THE SITE

It can be particularly daunting to be faced with a neglected piece of ground, usually infested with weeds. A good way to tackle the work is to divide it into four areas for rotating annual crops, plus one for more permanent planting with rhubarb, herbs and soft

ABOVE LEFT: This plot is ready for digging over. It has full sun for most of the day as well as shelter from strong winds.

OPPOSITE: This attractive plot is in a sunny spot against a brick wall.

These established vegetable plots have open aspects and are on slight slopes, providing good drainage and plenty of light.

fruits. Crop rotation is important to reduce the build-up of pests and diseases in the soil. The various crops use up nutrients differently so soil can become depleted if the same ones are grown repeatedly in the same spot.

On restricted sites, or where there is a more relaxed attitude to growing, a system of polyculture can be followed where there is no formal division of beds. Permaculture is the development of ecosystems intended to be sustainable and self-sufficient, the position of crops being determined by the maturing and harvesting of the previous ones.

Make a path through the centre of the plot, wide enough to accommodate a wheelbarrow and edged with gravel boards or scaffolding planks. If the site is fairly level, landscape fabric can be used, which acts as a barrier between soil and the preferred top mulch, preventing soil migration and ensuring a clean attractive surface. Then use more landscape fabric to make side paths running at right-angles to the main one, pinning it down with wire

BACKYARD FARMING

OPPOSITE: This newly-dug patch has had gravel paths added to separate the various crops and allow easy access for sowing and weeding.

BELOW: As plots are dug over, weeds are eliminated and organic matter can be added.

hoops or plastic pegs. These can be moved to accommodate different planting configurations and to make cultivation easier.

Paths will also reduce the amount or trampling on the beds, so they may not need to be dug over again, apart from some light forking, to turn in some manure. This forms the basis of the no dig method of gardening, where the organic matter is scattered over the surface and becomes incorporated during planting and by the action of worms in the soil.

One of the problems with developing a plot from a weedy condition, or from pasture, is that there may be more pests than usual, such as leatherjackets and wireworms. These pests live on the roots of plants so that

when the weeds are removed they will turn their attention to your crops instead. When cultivating the soil, destroy any pests you find, a task in which you will find the birds will help and even keep you company as you work. There will also be a reservoir of weed seeds which will take quite a few years to be depleted. Some can remain viable for over 20 years, but their

numbers will decline if they are not allowed to mature.

It is probably best to plant in rows running in a north–south direction, which gives maximum light and fewer shadows. Sheds or greenhouses, if they are to be included, should be placed at the northern end to avoid shading of the plot. Should there be trees, large shrubs or a hedge nearby,

their roots may extend into the plot, which will mean a loss of moisture and nutrients and the crops will suffer as a result. Smaller roots, which reach beyond the canopy, can be severed to lessen the problem, but larger supporting roots cannot, so you may need to choose another site. Once roots have been removed, however, a vertical barrier should prevent them from encroaching again.

The diagram (left) is a suggested layout for the first year. This will entail the addition of well-rotted manure or compost in Area 1, as potatoes will require plenty of moisture and nutrition. (Courgettes/zucchini and sweetcorn are also gross feeders, so can be grown in this plot as well.) If the plot is large, this may be the only area tackled in the first year, with a little work done on the remainder. Cover any undeveloped areas with landscape fabric or old carpet laid upside-down

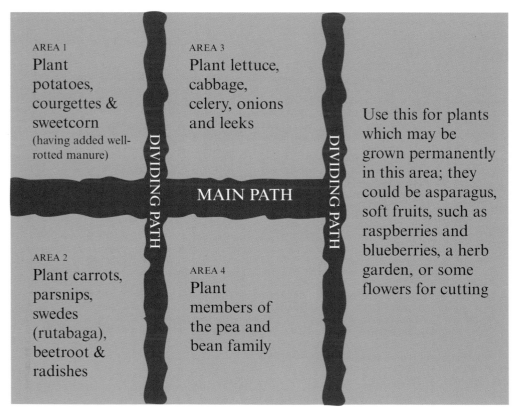

AREA 1
Plant potatoes, courgettes & sweetcorn (having added well-rotted manure)

AREA 3
Plant lettuce, cabbage, celery, onions and leeks

DIVIDING PATH

MAIN PATH

DIVIDING PATH

Use this for plants which may be grown permanently in this area; they could be asparagus, soft fruits, such as raspberries and blueberries, a herb garden, or some flowers for cutting

AREA 2
Plant carrots, parsnips, swedes (rutabaga), beetroot & radishes

AREA 4
Plant members of the pea and bean family

to block out the light; this will kill existing weeds and prevent others from germinating, making it easier to cultivate later on. In subsequent years the rest of the plot will be subjected to double digging (see page 27) as the crops rotate until they are back at the start after the fourth year, when the organic matter can be spread on the surface and incorporated with a digging fork. With a smaller plot, the whole can be dug over at once before dividing it into the different crop areas, at the same time incorporating organic matter in the relevant areas.

Most people would prefer to grow food without resorting to chemicals, but by suspending this good practice for a few weeks, the clearing of a new plot can be made less effortful by using a total weedkiller, which can be obtained from any garden store. This will destroy weeds and their roots, without leaving a residue in the soil, so that the ground can be used once clearing is complete. To ensure total removal, leave the plot for a while to ensure that the more stubborn weeds are truly dead, repeating the procedure should they recover. This method may

A neat row of onions.

take longer than digging out the weeds, but it is more thorough and much easier on the back!

Once weeds have been removed, dig over the area with a fork, removing remaining weed roots and large stones. To add manure, remove a trench of soil to a depth of two spits (i.e. double the length of a spade's blade) at one end, moving it to just beyond the far end. Dig the manure into the bottom of this trench, being careful not to bring the subsoil up into the top layer, then turn the next row of spits on top of this. Repeat this along the area, incorporating more manure as you go and covering it with the turned-over soil until the end is reached, when the soil from the first trench is used to fill in the last. This is the process known as double digging. If the ground has been

OPPOSITE: Brassicas, such as cabbages and kale, can be grown together.

RIGHT: Here, alfalfa (a leguminous plant) is being grown as a green manure, which will eventually be dug into the soil to add nutrients and organic matter. Alfalfa contains nitrogen-fixing symbiotic bacteria in its root nodules that fix atmospheric nitrogen in a form that plants can readily use.

cultivated before or is easy to work, the double digging can be performed during the clearing operation.

This may seem like hard work, but the resulting bed will yield excellent production for years. If you are not accustomed to this kind of work, then it should be tackled in small segments over a number of weeks when the weather is suitable. The rest of the plot can be treated in the same way later on or the following year, depending on its size and the gardener's energy level.

The following year use Area 2 for the potatoes, with the addition of

manure. In the second year, Area 1 is used for other root vegetables, such as carrots, swedes (rutabaga), parsnips, beetroot and radishes, which do better in ground that has not recently been manured. The potatoes move to Areas 3 and 4 in subsequent years, then start again in Area 1. This time the area does not require double digging as manure can be dug into the bottom of the trench in which the 'seed' potatoes are to be planted. Thus the four-year cycle begins again and proceeds in the same manner (Crops to be planted in the rotation are as indicated in the diagram

on page 24.) This is the ideal cropping arrangement, but preparation of the plot means that it may not become established for a few years.

A simpler rotation can be followed on a three-year cycle by including the potatoes with the root crops or leaving them out altogether if space does not permit. The crops are for the individual to choose, but those listed are the ones most commonly used.

The permanent planting areas can be placed at the northern end to reduce shading of the plot. The choice of crops depends on taste and the size of the area available, but are the ones

which remain for a number of years, with strawberries lasting for about three years and asparagus for up to 20. Preparation is the same as for the rest of the plot. In subsequent years the area should be mulched with manure to

ABOVE: Raking in well-rotted manure.

LEFT: Table showing the amount of lime in grams to be added per square metre to different soil types to achieve a pH of about 6–6.5.

OPPOSITE: A perfectly dug bed with neatly-mounded drills.

pH of soil	Sandy soil g/sq m	Loamy soil g/sq m	Clay soil g/sq m
4.5	190	285	400
5.0	155	235	330
5.5	130	190	260
6.0	118	155	215

keep weeds down, leaving the worms to work it into the soil. The non-cultivation or no-dig method of crop-growing uses this technique over the whole plot. The soil is not dug: instead, a thick mulch of compost or rotted manure is laid on the soil and the crops are planted through it. The initial preparation to clear the site is the same as before, as no amount of mulching will stop perennial weeds.

If there are periods when an area is not in production, for example, after harvesting a crop, it should be covered with a thick mulch of compost or with landscape fabric to prevent weeds from germinating; do not use plastic sheeting as it does not allow air in and the soil will become stagnant. The compost will be taken into the soil by worms, so eliminating the need to dig to incorporate it the following spring.

Another use for fallow areas is to grow a green manure. This is an annual crop, such as mustard (spring or summer sowing) or alfalfa (late summer or autumn sowing). It will prevent soil erosion, smother weeds and improve the soil structure. Before the plants mature and still have plenty of sap, they are removed, left to wilt, then turned into the soil, roots and all, at

least two to three weeks before re-planting, so that they are completely buried and left to break down, returning their nutrients to the soil. The soil structure is better maintained when it is being used with growing roots keeping it open; a plot left barren, with nothing growing (even weeds), will soon become compacted and stagnant.

Other green manures, which can be grown in winter, are corn salad (lamb's lettuce) or field (fava) beans, which have shallow roots and are easily incorporated. Keep to the principles of crop rotation by using varieties related to the harvested crop, for example, field beans after peas/beans and mustard after brassicas. Phacelia is not related to any vegetable so can be used after any crop. Some of the seed sold for the purpose is used by commercial growers who use heavy machinery to incorporate the deeper roots and are not so suitable for garden use.

If the soil is not of a chalky nature it will tend to become acid as the calcium in the soil is leached out. Moreover, the addition of compost and manure tends to lower the pH (power of hydrogen). Consequently it may require

OPPOSITE & BELOW: Raised beds are ideal for small areas or where the existing soil is poor.

the addition of lime from time to time as most vegetables grow best when the soil pH is between 5.5 and 7; this is because some of the nutrients become unavailable to plants beyond this range. It is preferable to do a pH test taking soil from several areas of the plot to work out the amount of lime to add to achieve this optimum level (see page 28).

Use ordinary lime (calcium carbonate), this being less caustic than quicklime (calcium oxide). Choose a calm day, marking out the area in 1m² strips, and sprinkle the lime evenly before digging it in. This is best done well before planting to avoid scorching roots and should not be applied at the same time as fertilizer or manure to avoid the loss of nitrogen; a chemical reaction causes ammonia to form, which is gaseous and escapes into the atmosphere. Late autumn or winter is traditionally the time when liming is carried out.

Raised Beds
These have been in use for centuries and with good reason: they're not only better for all the vegetables you intend

to grow but, being at a more comfortable level, where a gardener's anatomy is concerned, they reduce the aches and pains produced by kneeling or bending over. The beds can be built using wood, landscaping ties, decorative paving slabs, or stone, with or without mortar (use your imagination where other materials are concerned). They should be no wider than 4ft (1.2m) so that plants growing in the middle can be reached from both sides. Raised beds exceeding 10ft (3m) in length will require additional stakes in the middle of the two long sides.

This is to keep them from bowing out under the weight of the soil should the sides be made of a flimsier material.

Raised garden beds are especially useful where space is limited, as the spacings between plants can be reduced. Building them is an easy task and they can also be purchased ready-made, there being a variety of quality modular beds available in kit form. Railway sleepers are also available and are excellent for this purpose.

Raised beds make it easier to introduce a rich and balanced growing medium. Fill them with the soil of your

choice, then add plenty of well-rotted manure or compost, maintaining and adding to this over time.

Soil conditions and types can be controlled more efficiently and can be varied from bed to bed. Moreover, the soil does not get compacted because it is not walked upon; remember, soil needs water and air to function, and compaction robs it of both. Therefore soils that aren't compacted have a greater ability to hold plant-available water, form fewer clods, permit greater root growth and give higher plant yields as a result. Remember also that soil compaction has the potential to reduce yields by up to 50 per cent.

Other advantages of raised bed systems are:

- their tendency to drain away excess moisture better than ordinary garden beds
- the soil warms up quicker in the spring
- there is no need to dig beds over
- they are easier to keep weed- and pest-free
- frames for covers can easily be devised

TOOLS AND EQUIPMENT
You will need the correct tools for the job before starting work on your vegetable patch.

SPADE Used to dig or loosen ground or to break up clumps of soil.

FORK Used for loosening, lifting and turning over the soil.

HOE Used to weed and groom the soil around shallow-rooted plants, also to chop off annual weeds (perennial weeds must be dug and removed) and plants at ground level. Can also be used to

Tools for the job: a rake and hoe (opposite), a trowel and gardening gloves (right).

LEFT: Forks and spades are the gardener's most important tools.

BELOW: To avoid forgetting, use plastic labels to mark spots where seeds have been sown.

OPPOSITE ABOVE LEFT: Store tools indoors where they are always conveniently to hand.

OPPOSITE ABOVE RIGHT: Seed trays can be kept and re-used from year to year.

OPPOSITE BELOW: A wheelbarrow is useful for moving heavy objects.

create narrow drills (furrows) and shallow trenches for planting seeds and generally to dig and move soil (e.g.

GREENHOUSES AND OTHER FORMS OF
PLANT PROTECTION
Prevailing climatic conditions affect the
types of plants suitable for growing in
different parts of the world; therefore,
it makes sense to grow those that are
most suited to your own particular

harvesting potatoes), and chop weeds,
roots and crop residues.

RAKE Used for removing waste
material, such as dug-up weeds and
stones, from the surface of the soil.

TROWEL Used for breaking up soil,
digging small holes – especially for
planting and weeding – mixing in
fertilizer or other additives, and
transferring plants to pots.

WHEEBARROW Used for moving soil,
plants and other heavy garden objects
from place to place.

environment. But where the serious gardener is concerned, the greenhouse is a more than useful addition, in that it permits a wider range of plants to be grown, and also produces them earlier than the seasonal norm. If all you wish to do, however, is raise a few seedlings and cuttings, cloches, cold frames, conservatories and old-fashioned sunporches may be sufficient for this purpose, although none of these offers quite the same amount of dedicated growing space as the true greenhouse.

SHELTER

One of the most important things a greenhouse can do is provide additional warmth and protection from the elements, and there is one particular aspect of this role which is often forgotten. While cold frames and mini-greenhouses manage this very effectively for plants, they provide little or no shelter for the gardener. To steal a march, by bringing on plants during the cold, wet days of winter, is an attractive idea but not a particularly practical one without protection from the worst that winter has to offer.

But with a door to shut behind you, pottering about and checking how things are progressing suddenly becomes a more pleasant prospect, and with power, heat and light laid on, the useful hours that can be spent there can be greatly extended. While staying warm and dry is obviously relevant to us all, it may be of particular benefit

Greenhouses give plants a head start and permit a much longer growing season.

to the elderly or infirm. Nor is it only the gardener who gains; working with a cold frame open, the plants can get chilled, but in a greenhouse they are as well-protected as the gardener himself.

GROWING OPPORTUNITIES

The greenhouse encourages us to grow at least some of our own food – also bedding plants. All manner of fruit and vegetables lend themselves to being grown even in unheated conditions – and the choice is not limited to tomatoes alone. Apart from the old greenhouse favourites, strawberries, chillies, peppers, aubergines (eggplants), peaches, nectarines and even grapes can all be raised successfully, provided suitable varieties are chosen, while the addition of some heat, during the colder months, makes even wider choices possible.

A final aspect, that tends to be overlooked, is the real contribution a greenhouse makes to the garden as a whole. Not only does it allow plants to be produced at a fraction of the cost of buying them, but there is also more satisfaction to be had from doing this, while a well-managed greenhouse can be regarded an art form in itself.

COMPOSTING

No backyard farmer should be without some form of composter. Whether it be a heap in a corner or a more complicated arrangement, it is a place where suitable material can be left to rot down.

Composting is an excellent way to upcycle kitchen and garden waste into an extremely useful humus-like soil product, which permits the return to the soil of vital organic matter,

Provided it is well-maintained, a greenhouse can be an attractive and useful addition to any backyard plot.

nutrients, and bacteria in particular, that are vital to plant nutrition.

Composting biodegrades organic matter, and is performed by micro-organisms, mostly bacteria, but also by yeasts and fungi. The composting process produces an end-product that is dark, crumbly, and sweet-smelling.

ADDING ORGANIC MATERIALS TO A COMPOST BIN

Micro-organisms, such as bacteria and fungi, break sown the soft material. This causes the compost to heat to around 140°F (60°C), which is the ideal temperature for micro-organisms to do their job. The compost then cools to below 70°F (30°C), when small creatures, such as worms and insects, then break down the tougher material. The whole process usually takes about 3–9 months, and results in a nutrient-rich material to return to your garden. The compost that is ready to use can be taken from the bottom of the pile, leaving the rest to complete the process.

A composter is an essential element in every situation where plants are raised. It is good for the environment, upcycling waste matter to return nutrients to the soil.

COMPOST BINS

Manufactured bins include plastic ones, turning units, hoops, cones, and stacking bins. Home-made bins can be constructed out of scrap wood, chicken wire, fencing or even old garbage cans, with holes punched into the sides and base. A simple wooden bin can be made by creating a frame out of wood and attaching it to the ground by means of corner posts. It should have a capacity of about 50–80 gallons (200-300 litres), and should ideally have a lid to keep out rain. The bin should be placed in a sunny spot out of the wind. Improve drainage by first breaking up the soil beneath the compost bin.

CHAPTER TWO

GROWING VEGETABLES

SOWING AND PLANTING

Before sowing, certain seeds may require a prior treatment, such as scarification, stratification, soaking, or cleaning using cold or medium–hot water. Seeds can either be sown broadcast or in drills. Sowing broadcast means scattering the seeds on the surface of the soil, and sowing in drills means setting seeds in soil in orderly rows. Sowing in rows is particularly appropriate where vegetables are concerned, and where many different kinds will be grown, each one, preferably, in a row of its own.

Before sowing seeds, the ground needs to be prepared by digging it over with a spade to make sure there are no large lumps of soil or stones, then raking over the surface to make a seedbed with a fine 'tilth', which is when the soil is sufficiently broken down into fine particles, that will not impede the passage of the tiny seeds as they germinate and begin to push up through the surface of the soil.

Planting is simply putting an existing plant or bulb into soil, that is appropriate for the individual plant, to allow it to grow and develop. Make a hollow in the soil where you wish to plant, then place the root ball of the plant into the hollow, filling it in with soil. Using your hands, press the soil around the stem so that the root ball is firmly anchored, ensuring that the roots make good contact with the soil.

To transplant is to transfer seedlings, grown in a seedbed, to the actual site where the plants are required to grow on. This not only toughens the plants but also stimulates growth.

DRILLS To sow in drills, dig over the soil, rake it, then mark out rows with a stick or the back of a hoe. Sow the seeds in the rows, then cover the seeds by raking the soil from the sides of the row over the drill. Water gently. Small seeds are usually sprinkled evenly along the row, while large seeds, such as peas or beans, are usually sown singly a few inches apart. If the seedlings come up too thickly to allow the plants room to grow properly, you will need to thin them out by removing the unwanted, weaker seedlings.

SEEDBEDS Specific areas where seeds are sown for germination. The area is preferably level and with a fine soil which helps the young plants to break through and makes it easy to lift them for planting out. The seedlings may be left to grow to adult plants in the seedbed, perhaps after thinning them to remove the weaker ones, or they may be moved elsewhere as young plants.

These raised areas are used as seedbeds to produce seedlings that will later be transplanted into the main vegetable plot.

GROWING VEGETABLES

Some of the following are not vegetables, in the true sense of the word, but most people would consider and use them as such.

Aubergines (Eggplants) see Chillies etc.

BEANS, BROAD (FAVA BEANS)

Prepare the soil well in advance; it should have been well-dug and treated with manure the previous winter. Seeds are best sown outdoors in open ground, the usual time being from March to May, but if the climate is mild, the soil is well-drained and there is natural shelter, seeds may be sown in November. Sow beans 2 inches (5 centimetres) deep, with 8in (20cm) between seeds, in rows 24in (60cm) apart. There should be no need to thin out the seedlings. Beans sown in autumn (fall) will be ready in 26 weeks, those that have been spring-sown in about 14 weeks.

Alternatively, if a greenhouse, cold frame or cool window sill is available, it is possible to sow seeds in deep seed trays or modules. They will take about 14 days to germinate and should be ready to plant out in early March for harvesting in late May and June.

BEANS, FRENCH & KIDNEY

The soil should be well-dug, slightly acid, moisture-retentive and well-manured. The seeds may be sown in April in protective cloches, or in late May or early June in open ground. Remove cloches in late May. Sow the seeds in 2-in (5-cm) deep drills, one bean every 4in (10cm), with about 18in (45cm) between rows. Support the plants as they grow with short twigs or bean sticks, using longer canes or netting for climbing varieties. The beans will be ready for harvesting in 8–12 weeks.

ABOVE & RIGHT: Kidney beans.

OPPOSITE: French beans.

BEETROOT (BEETS)

Beets prefer an unshaded spot in a light sandy soil, the soil having been limed if acid. The seeds may be sown outdoors in open ground or started off in pots at least 8in (20cm) wide. For an early crop (late May), sow the seeds in pots in February, keeping them above 55°F (13°C). From mid April onwards, the seeds may be sown directly into a prepared seedbed. Continue to sow new batches of seed every month to extend the cropping period up to the end of June.

To speed germination, soak the seeds in tepid water for 24 hours, sowing the seeds while they are still wet. The first seedlings should appear within 10–14 days. If originally sown in pots, plant out when the beets are about 4in (10cm) high, hardening off the plants over two weeks; for early crops plant them out initially under polythene or cloches. Allow 2in (5cm) between plants with 12in (30cm) between rows.

In open ground, sow two seeds together about 1in (2.5cm) deep, 2in (5cm) apart with 12in (30cm) between rows. When the seedlings are about an inch high, thin out the weaker where

both seeds have germinated, discarding the thinnings. Harvest 11–16 weeks after planting.

To store late-cropping beetroots, lift on a dry day in October, leaving the beets on the surface of the soil to dry. Twist off, rather than cut off, the leaves to avoid bleeding. Place in dry sand in trays, making sure the beets are not touching one another, and store in a cool, frost-free place. In mild areas, where the soil is not susceptible to waterlogging, beets can be left in the ground provided they are protected from frost.

BROCCOLI and CALABRESE

Broccoli prefers an unshaded, rich, moisture-retentive soil to which lime has been added if the soil is acid, but which has not been freshly manured (best done the previous autumn). Never add lime and manure at the same time because they react together and benefit neither. By adding manure in autumn and lime in spring, sufficient time will have elapsed to prevent trouble. Avoid planting in an area where the previous crop belonged to the brassica family (i.e., cabbage, swede/rutabaga, rape, mustard, etc.). Sow seeds outdoors in a seedbed in late April to May, sowing the seeds very thinly in ½-in (1.2-cm) deep drills with about 6in (15cm) spacing in between.

Thin the seedlings as they grow, increasing spacings between the plants to about 3in (7.5cm). When seedlings

are about 3in high (June or July), transplant them to their final growing position. Water the day before lifting, then plant firmly about an inch deeper than they were when growing in the seedbed, allowing spacings between plants of about 12in (30cm) for green-sprouting varieties, 18in (45cm) for purple and white varieties.

The time from sowing to harvest is about 12 weeks for the green-sprouting varieties, and about 44 weeks for the purple or white varieties, which take longer to mature.

OPPOSITE & ABOVE: Green-sprouting broccoli.

RIGHT: A purple-sprouting variety.

BRUSSELS SPROUTS

Brussels sprouts like an unshaded, rich and moisture-retentive soil to which lime has been added if the soil is acid. Do not add fresh manure, which is best done the previous autumn. Avoid planting in an area where the previous crop also belonged to the brassica family. Sow seeds outdoors in a seedbed in early March under cloches or from late March to mid April without. Sow the seeds very thinly in drills ½in (1.2cm) deep, allowing about 6in (15cm) between rows.

As the seedlings grow, thin them out to about 3in (7.5cm) apart. Once the plants are 4–6in (10–15cm) high (late May/early June), transplant them to their final growing position. Water the seedbed the day before lifting, then plant the seedlings in rows, their lowest leaves just above the soil level, spacing the plants about 2½ft (75cm) apart. The time from sowing to harvest is between 28 weeks (early varieties) and 36 weeks (late varieties).

CABBAGES

SPRING CABBAGE Sow the seeds outdoors in a seedbed, preferably in unshaded, rich and moisture-retentive soil to which lime has been added if the soil is acid. Do not add fresh manure (best done the previous autumn). Avoid planting in an area where the previous crop was one of the brassica family. Sowing time is late July to early August. Sow the seeds very thinly in drills ½in (1.2cm) deep with about 6in (15cm) between rows.

Thin out seedlings to about 3in (7.5cm) apart.

Once the plants have five or six leaves (late September/early August), transplant them to their final growing position. Water the seedbed the day before lifting, then plant the seedlings

slightly deeper than they were in the seedbed in rows about 6in (15cm) apart, with about 12in (30cm) between rows. Alternatively, the plants may be thinned in March to provide spring greens. The time from sowing to harvest is about 35 weeks.

SUMMER CABBAGE Sow the seeds in a seedbed outdoors, preferably in an unshaded, rich and moisture-retentive soil, to which lime has been added if the soil is acid. No not add fresh manure (best done the previous autumn). Avoid planting in areas where other brassicas were previously grown. Sowing time is from late March to early May. Sow seeds very thinly in drills ½in (1.2cm) deep with about 6in (15cm) between rows. As the seedlings grow, thin them out to about 3in (7.5cm) apart.

Once the plants have five or six leaves (May or June), transplant them to their final growing position. Water the seedbed the day before lifting, then plant the seedlings, slightly deeper than they were when in the seedbed, in rows about 12in (30cm) apart with about 12in between rows. The time from sowing to harvest is about 20–35 weeks.

LEFT: Red cabbage.

OPPOSITE: Savoy cabbage.

WINTER AND SAVOY CABBAGES Sow the seeds in seedbeds outdoors, preferably in unshaded, rich and moisture-retentive soil, to which lime has been added if the soil is acid. Do not add fresh manure (best done the previous autumn). Avoid areas where brassicas were previously grown.

Sowing time is from late March to early May. Sow the seeds very thinly in drills ½in (1.2cm) deep, with about 6in (15cm) between rows. As the seedlings grow, thin them out to about 3in (7.5cm) apart.

Once the plants have five or six leaves (July), transplant them to their final growing position. Water the seedbed the day before lifting, then plant the seedlings slightly deeper than they were when in the seedbed, in rows about 12in (30cm) apart with about 12in between rows. The time from sowing to harvest is about 20–35 weeks.

CARROTS

Home-grown carrots may not look as perfect as the ones produced for supermarkets, but they have infinitely more flavour. Carrots prefer a light, stone-free soil. Never sow seeds onto freshly manured soil. Sow outdoors in open ground in early March under cloches or without cloches from March to the end of June. Sow the seeds very thinly in ½-in (1.2-cm) deep drills with about 8in (20cm) between rows. As the seedlings grow, thin them out to about 3in (7.5cm) apart. Discard the thinnings, which do not transplant well, and which will attract carrot root fly if left on the soil. The time from sowing to harvest is about 12 weeks for baby carrots and about 16 weeks for main-crop.

To store late-cropping carrots, lift them, cut off the foliage, and bury them in dry sand in trays, making sure the carrots are not touching one another. Store in a dark, cool but frost-free place.

In areas where the soil is not susceptible to waterlogging, the foliage can be removed and the carrots left in the ground, provided they are protected from frost.

CAULIFLOWER

Avoid freshly manured soil (the excessive nitrogen will make the growth leafy at the expense of producing florets). Sow outdoors in a seedbed in a slightly acid (pH 6) soil. Sow the seeds very thinly, from late March to early May, in drills ½-in (1.2-cm) deep with about 6in (15cm) between rows. As the seedlings grow, thin them out to about 3in (7.5cm) apart.

Once the plants have five or six leaves (late June/July), transplant them to their final growing position. Water

the seedbed the day before lifting, then plant the seedlings in rows at the same level as they were in the seedbed. Space the plants 2ft (60cm) apart for summer and autumn varieties, and 2½ft (75cm) apart for winter varieties. The time from sowing to harvest is 18–24 weeks for summer and autumn varieties, and 40–50 weeks for winter varieties.

CELERY

The ideal environment for growing celery is one where there are no weather or temperature extremes. Seeds may be sown outdoors once all risk of a frost occurring has passed. The soil must be well-prepared by digging it over, removing stones and weeds and mixing in a well-rotted manure. A light sprinkling of general-purpose granular fertilizer may be raked in around a week before planting out seedlings.

Plants may be started off by sowing seeds during March and April. Fill a tray or pot with seed compost, levelling it and allowing it to settle. Celery seed is particularly fine and difficult to handle, but should be sown lightly across the surface of the compost (it may be easier to take a pinch of seed at a time). Water by standing the tray or pot in a larger tray of water, allowing the water to soak up into the compost rather than disturbing the seeds by watering from the top. Cover with a thin layer of vermiculite and place the tray or pot in a location where there is constant warmth, a heated propagator on a window sill or a greenhouse being ideal for the task. Keep the compost moist, never letting

it dry out. If a propagator is used, remove the seedlings once they have germinated and formed leaves. Pot them on, using 3-in pots filled with multi-purpose compost. Water the plants in. After five weeks, or when the seedlings have reached 3–4in (8–10cm) in height, the plants can be hardened off in a cold frame or sheltered outdoor location. In May or June, when weather conditions permit, plant them on into their final position.

Plant out the seedlings in deep trenches, with the crown of each plant at ground level. Leave a space of 10–12in (25–30cm) between plants, and arrange them in a grid rather than a row for best results. Water plants in thoroughly.

Celery is usually harvested from August onwards until the first autumn frosts. Once the celery has reached the required size, harvest it either by cutting off the plant just above the soil line, taking all the stalks together as one head, or harvest the outer stalks leaving the inner ones intact. Wash the stalk bulb or stalks and dry. Stored in the fridge the celery will last for two weeks. It will blanch naturally.

Watering regularly and frequently is the key to producing good celery.

Keep the plants weed-free to avoid competition for nutrients and moisture. Feed once with a liquid fertilizer at around four weeks after planting out to help the celery along.

Although celery will blanch naturally after it is picked, and some varieties are self-blanching, some gardeners blanch the stalks while they are growing in order to reduce bitterness and to produce the desirable pale stems. Soil or mulch built up around the stalks, around four weeks before harvesting, will produce this result.

CHILLIES, SWEET PEPPERS & AUBERGINES (EGGPLANTS)

Chillies, sweet peppers and aubergines (eggplants) are usually regarded as crops for warmer climates, but further north they can be grown successfully under glass or in polytunnels. All need a long season to mature, so have the seeds planted in small pots by the end of February or middle of March and into their final growing spots (or pots) by June, by which time they can also be grown outdoors, provided that the winter frosts are well and truly over. All three of these delicious crops are grown in the same way and there are plenty of great varieties from which to choose.

Full sun and a soil rich in organic material will provide the best growing conditions for all three, and patios, roof gardens or balconies are ideal locations where they can catch the sun.

Growing from seed and planting out is identical in each case. To start them off, fill pots (ideally 3in/7–8cm deep) with seed compost, gently firming it down and levelling off the tops. Scatter a thin layer of seeds over the surface; don't sow too many, as most of the seeds will germinate.

Sprinkle over a fine layer of vermiculite, then water in.

What you do next depends on the space and resources at your disposal. To encourage germination, a constant temperature of around 70°F (21°C) needs to be maintained, for which a special heat pad, propagator – or for a more makeshift arrangement, a window sill above a radiator – will suffice. The pots can also be covered with polythene bags. Germination will vary between one and three weeks depending on varieties. Once the seedlings appear, start to reduce the temperature

OPPOSITE: Red chillies.

ABOVE & RIGHT: Sweet peppers.

gradually, continuing to ensure that the plants do not dry out. Transplant the seedlings into pots of their own when they have grown a second set of leaves. Do this carefully, loosening the compost and gently lifting the seedlings out, without touching the roots. The same pots as before can be used, but this time allow only one seedling per pot. Use a multi-purpose compost, levelled and tapped down, and with a dibber make a hole, planting the seedling with its leaves just above the surface. Place the plants in a greenhouse, conservatory or on a sunny window sill. When the roots start to come out of the drainage holes, it is time to move the plants into larger 5-in (12–13-cm) pots.

Plants can go outside once all risk of frost has passed, first hardening them off for a few days by placing them outside only during the day. Peppers and chillies can be grown on in 1.3-gallon (5-litre) containers, but aubergines do better if they can be got into the ground, either in a greenhouse or polytunnel. Water chillies, aubergines and peppers regularly and also mist the plants to maintain a damp atmosphere. If you do not have a warm, sunny and sheltered spot outside, these plants are best kept permanently under glass.

Harvesting is between late June and September: use a knife or scissors to remove the fruit. Sweet peppers mature from green to red; chillies can be picked

LEFT: Bell peppers.

OPPOSITE: Aubergines.

high-nitrogen fertilizers; this will only result in very leafy plants with few fruit.

Chillies, peppers and aubergines are very thirsty plants, so never allow their compost to dry out; in hot weather, water several times a day, as steady growth without check will produce the best crops.

Aubergines are subject to red spider and whitefly. Dampness will ward off red spider, and whitefly can be sprayed or removed using a vacuum cleaner (if you shake the plant, the flies will take off and you can catch them on the wing). Most varieties of sweet pepper are now disease-resistant.

Corn (see Sweetcorn)

Courgettes/Zucchini (see Vegetable Marrow)

and used when green or left to redden and mature. Pick aubergines when they have reached the optimum size for the variety, and when the fruit has assumed its characteristic glossy appearance. An aubergine plant will produce up to five fruits. When autumn arrives, remove the plants and hang them up to allow the remaining fruit to continue ripening.

If necessary, use sticks or canes to support the plants once they reach 8in (20cm) or so; it is a good idea to pinch out growing tips to encourage a bushier plant with more fruit. If grown in a container, plants will need to be given a liquid feed throughout the season. A tomato fertilizer is suitable for the purpose, but any liquid feed with a high potash content may be used. Don't use

CUCUMBERS

Sow seeds indoors in pots of compost or outdoors in open ground. If outdoors, choose a sheltered site in summer (light shade is tolerated) with moisture-retentive, humus-rich soil.

Sow mid April if starting plants off indoors. Using 2–3-in (5–7.5-cm) pots filled with seed compost, sow two seeds on their edges per pot, at a depth of ½in (1.2cm), removing the weaker seedling at a later stage. Harden off the seedlings, planting them out from late May to early June, with 15–18in (38–45cm) spacings between plants for climbing varieties, and 30in (75cm) for trailing varieties. Plant out seedlings at intervals to provide a succession of cucumbers, while pinching out the growing tips of the plants after six or seven leaves have developed will encourage fruiting on the side shoots.

Sow seeds outdoors from May to early June. Sow two or three seeds together, on their edges, at a depth of 1in (2.5cm) under cloches or glass jars, allowing 15–18in (38–45cm) between groups if a climbing variety, or 30in (75cm) between groups if a trailing variety. Remove the weaker seedlings at a later stage. Pinching out the growing tips of the plants after six or seven leaves have developed will encourage fruiting on side shoots.

Eggplants (Aubergines) see Chillies etc.

LEEKS

Leeks prefer an open site that has been well-dug and preferably manured the previous autumn. Alternatively, garden compost or well-rotted manure can be incorporated before planting.

For main-crop leeks, sow seed from late March to April, directly into a seedbed about 1.2cm (½ inch) deep in rows about 15cm (6 inch) apart.

Once the seeds have germinated and shoots are visible, thin out the seedlings, spacing them about 3.7cm (1½ inch) apart.

Transplant the seedlings in June or early July when they are about 8in (20cm) long and of a similar thinness as a pencil. Water the bed the day before lifting if the earth is dry. Use a dibber to make holes about 9in (23cm) apart in the main bed, and plant each seedling into a hole.

The time from sowing to harvesting is about 30 weeks for early varieties and about 45 weeks for late varieties.

LETTUCES

Use light, friable, well-drained soil, to which lime has been added if the soil is acid, and which has recently had organic matter added. Sow seeds from late March to July, in seedbeds or in open ground. Sow the seeds very thinly in ½-in (1.2-cm) deep drills, leaving about 6in (15cm) between rows in seedbeds or 10–12in (25–30cm) between rows in open ground. Successive small sowings will extend the lettuce harvest without producing a glut.

As they grow, thin the seedlings in open ground to about 6–12in

(15–20cm) apart, depending on the variety; transplant the seedlings from the seedbed when the plants are about 2in (5cm) high, planting them in rows with about 6–12in in between, depending on the variety, and with 10–12in (25–30cm) between rows. The time from sowing to harvesting is 6–14 weeks depending on the variety.

Marrows (see Vegetable Marrows etc.)

Lettuce comes in many forms, including butterhead (bibb), romaine or cos, and the green and red oak-leaf varieties.

ONIONS

Using onion sets, rather than seeds, is an easier option where the beginner is concerned, and even experienced growers often prefer growing onions this way. Sets are immature onion bulbs and, as such, have more stored energy within them than seed. They are also more reliable, disease-resistant, and only slightly more expensive to buy than seed.

Plant onion sets in spring, two to four weeks before the last frosts, and use bulbs that are less than $3/4$in (19mm) diameter. Onion sets should be

spaced from 4–6in (10–15cm) apart, depending on the desired size of the mature bulbs. Press bulbs gently into the soil to about an inch (2.5cm) deep, so that their pointed tips just break the surface.

Sets can also be planted in September or October, which enables them to form strong seedlings that will overwinter and get off to a good start in spring. They usually provide a harvestable crop in June, which is a month or two earlier than spring-planted sets.

Many varieties, however, are not available as sets, and seed-grown onions seem to store better when harvested. You can, however, grow your own sets from seed, saving them to plant out the next season. Seeds can be started indoors and set in the soil as transplants or sown directly outside into the soil. Transplants may also be purchased in bunches from garden centres or seed catalogues, but they are expensive. Direct-seeding is impractical for long-season onions in most home situations, but is suitable for spring onions (scallions).

Onions are frost tolerant and like cool, wet spring weather. Being light feeders, they prefer rich, well-drained soil with a pH of 6.2–6.8. Onions are best grown in raised beds about 4in (10cm) high and 20in (50cm) wide, with 1–2in (2.5–5cm) of compost worked into the soil. Be sure to water consistently and keep weeds under control while onions are maturing.

Sow onion seeds very thinly in spring or autumn in ½-inch (1.2-cm) deep drills, leaving about 10–12in (25–30cm) between rows. The soil should be open, rich, well-drained, well-dug and lime added if acid. Do not sow onto a freshly manured bed, and avoid planting in an area where the previous crop was also a member of the onion family.

Thin spring-sown onion seedlings in stages to about 2–4in (5–10cm), being sure to remove all thinnings

(they may be used as spring onions or scallions) to prevent attack from onion fly. Thin autumn-sown seedlings to about 1in (2.5cm), making sure all thinnings are removed. In spring, further thin the seedlings to about 2–4in (5–10cm) between plants, remembering that closer spacings will give smaller onions than wider ones.

Onions must be thoroughly dried before storage. If the weather is fine, they may be laid on the surface of the soil to dry naturally, otherwise spread them out under cover. Once dry, remove the dead leaves before storing. Onions are ready for harvesting at around 22 weeks from the time of planting.

PARSNIPS

Parsnips require a long growing season, but they are available as a fresh vegetable throughout the winter, actually improving if frost gets to the roots. Parsnips will thrive in most deep, well-dug soils, to which lime has been added if the soil is acid, and should preferably have been manured for a previous crop.

To produce long, straight parsnips, the bed needs to be stone-free. Seeds may be sown outdoors in March, into ½-in (1.2-cm) deep drills, with about three seeds every 6in (15cm), and with rows about 12in (30cm) apart. Once seeds have germinated, and the shoots are visible, thin out to one seedling per position, discarding the thinnings.

To store late-cropping parsnips, lift the crop, remove the foliage, and store in dry sand in trays, ensuring that the parsnips are not touching one another. Store in a dark, cool but frost-free place.

In areas where the soil is not susceptible to waterlogging, the foliage may be cut off and the parsnips left in the ground until required, provided they are protected from frost.

PEAS

Peas sown in cold, wet ground are likely to rot off, so make sure the soil has had time to warm up sufficiently by covering it with polythene before sowing, and by later protecting the seedlings with fleece. Sow shorter varieties in a flat trench, 12in (30cm) deep and 10in (25cm) wide. Sow peas in open ground in light shade. It is essential that the soil is well-drained but moisture-retentive, and has been

deeply dug. Preferably it will have been manured the previous autumn. Sow seeds under cloches in late February or early March for a May/June crop, in late March/early April for a June/July crop, and in late June to early July for an autumn crop.

Sow peas in small trenches 6in (15cm) wide, 2in (5cm) deep and spaced to accommodate the expected height of the particular variety being grown; this will typically be 2–3ft (60–90cm) apart for short varieties, and 5–6ft (1.5–1.8m) apart for tall varieties

Press the pea seeds into the bottom of the drills in two rows along each side of each drill, with about 3in (7.5cm) between seeds, staggering the pea seeds in the rows. Cover with soil.

Support for the peas, in the form of netting, canes or trellises, depends on the variety being grown. Dwarf varieties (growing up to 18in/45cm high) normally require no support, but for the taller-growing varieties, strong support will be needed. Where necessary, this should be introduced when the seedlings are about 3in (7.5cm) high.

Peppers (see Chillies etc.)

POTATOES

It is useful to choose the right varieties for your culinary needs before you start. There are around 400 potato varieties available, and some are better than others for boiling, roasting, mashing, salads, etc.

Unlike most vegetables, potatoes prefer soil that is slightly acid, and they should be planted as far away as possible from places where lime has been applied. They are, however, greedy feeders, so a good amount of manure or compost, worked into the soil, will benefit them greatly as well as improve the texture of the soil.

There is no mystery attached to the process of chitting potatoes. All it means is that when you get your seed potatoes you put them in a cool but frost-free place where they get some light but not direct sunlight; near to a north-facing window in a frost-free shed would be ideal. The potatoes will then grow short, stubby shoots, which will get them off to a fast start when planted out. With Maincrop, some suggest rubbing off all but three shoots to get larger potatoes. Frost is the big enemy so you need to keep an eye on the weather. Usually mid March is about the right time to plant your Earlies, with Maincrop planted a few weeks later. If, after planting, the leaves (haulm) begin to show through and frost is threatening, the plants will need protection by bringing earth over from the sides to cover the haulm or by covering with fleece.

To plant, make a hole with a trowel and pop the seed potato in, or a trench may be drawn (take a draw hoe and scrape a trench) and the potatoes placed in it. Then soil is brought over from the sides to cover the potatoes.

Traditional planting distances are as follows:

First Earlies, Second Earlies and Salad varieties: 12in/30cm apart and 4in/10cm deep in rows 18in/45cm apart.

Maincrop varieties: 15in/40cm apart and 4in/10cm deep in rows 24in/60cm apart.

Maincrop types tend to store better but are at more risk of getting blight than the faster types, which are usually harvested before the blight periods begin.

As the plants grow, earth from the sides of the rows needs to be drawn up over the plants in a process known as earthing up. The potato tubers, which are the actual potatoes you will eventually eat, tend to grow towards the surface and they will turn green if light gets to them, making them unfit to eat, which is why earthing up these tubers is so important, and will also increase the crop. Remember, also, that covering up some of the leaves will not harm the plant or slow down its growth.

Potatoes are greedy feeders, so extra fertilizer needs to be added after a month or so when the plants are well-established. Use a specifically formulated potato fertilizer or an organic fertilizer such as fish, blood and bone. Good results can also be had from using a liquid comfrey feed which, in this form, makes itself immediately available to the plants.

In dry weather, keep the potatoes well-watered. If the water supply is irregular the yield will be reduced and the potatoes may suffer cracking from uneven growth.

New potatoes will be ready for harvesting at 8–12 weeks from the time of planting. Be aware that the longer potatoes are left in the ground the more they will mature, making them that much more susceptible to blight and other unwelcome pests and diseases.

RADISHES

Spring and autumn sowings may be made outdoors in open ground, but summer sowings require slight shade. Radishes enjoy a well-drained soil with plenty of humus added. Do not, however, sow on a freshly manured bed.

Summer varieties may be grown under cloches in January or February in mild areas, but cloches are not normally required once March is over. If winter varieties are preferred, sow from July–August.

Sow radish seeds in ½-in (1.2-cm) deep drills at intervals of about 1in

(2.5cm), leaving about 6in (15cm) between rows (for winter varieties, leave 9in/22cm between rows). Successive, small sowings of radish seeds, every two or three weeks, will extend the harvest without producing a glut. The time from sowing to harvesting is 3–6 weeks (summer varieties), 10–12 weeks (winter varieties).

Rutabaga (see Swedes)

SPINACH

Spinach is most often credited as being packed with iron, but it is also a rich source of vitamins A and C, thiamin, potassium and folic acid (one of the B-complex vitamins).

Spinach likes a moist but not waterlogged soil containing a good amount of organic matter. It does not like acid soils, and pH should be from 6.3–6.8. Sow seeds outdoors in open ground in early spring, or stagger the crop by sowing part rows every few weeks. The last sowing should be about 50–60 days before the first frosts. Winter varieties should be grown in open, unshaded, well-drained soil from August–September for harvesting from October–April. Sow seeds very thinly in 1-in (2.5-cm) deep drills about 12in (30cm) apart.

Thin the seedlings as they grow to provide space between plants of about 9in (23cm). Discard the thinnings – they will not transplant. To prolong cropping, pick off any seed heads as they appear. Time from sowing to harvest is from 8–14 weeks

Squashes (see Vegetable Marrows etc.)

SWEDES (RUTABAGA)

Similar to the turnip, but much easier to grow, the name is a contraction of 'swedish turnip'. Swedes, surprisingly, are members of the brassica family, therefore club root, which is a fungal disease, will be a problem if it is already in the soil: it is important that swedes are not grown on sites that have been used for other brassicas for at least two years.

Swedes are slow-growing vegetables, taking 20–26 weeks to reach maturity. They are hardy and best left in the ground over winter until required. Although they are harvested and stored as other root crops, they are at their best within a week of lifting.

Sow seeds outdoors in open ground, preferably in light, humus-rich soil with no tendency to dryness. Avoid acid soil, having added lime if required, and it should preferably have been manured for a previous crop.

Sow the seeds very thinly in ½–1-in (1.2–2.5-cm) deep drills about 15in (38cm) apart from late May to early June. Thin the seedlings, as they grow, to about 9in (23cm) between plants. Discard the thinnings – they will not transplant.

SWEETCORN (CORN)

Sweetcorn is deep-rooted and does not grow well in clay-based soils. Planting out in a large block is advisable, in that sweetcorn is wind-pollinated, and this will allow pollen from the male flowers to fall down onto the female tassels from which the cobs will grow.

Plant seeds out in April, putting out plug-grown plants in late May or June, in a location where there is full sun and shelter from strong winds. (Plug plants work well, transplanting easily and establishing quickly.)

To start seeds off indoors, fill 3-in (7.5-cm) pots with compost, making a 1-in (2–3-cm) deep hole in each with a dibber or the end of a pencil. Put two seeds in each hole, cover, and water. Leave the pots on a window sill to germinate. Remove the weaker seedling when growth of about an inch has been achieved. Place the pots outside in a shady location for a week or so to harden off before planting out.

Before planting out, dig out the intended bed deeply, mixing in well-rotted manure; ideally, this should have been done the previous autumn. Closer to the time of planting, remove weeds and large stones, digging over the ground. Level the ground and rake over. Make individual holes for each plant and gently firm them into the soil. Plant in blocks at least 13ft^2 (1.2m^2), leaving 12–14in (30–35cm) between plants and roughly 2ft (60cm) between rows. Use protective fleece in cold spells when the plants are still

vulnerable. Water regularly, especially once cobs begin to form. Take care, when using a Dutch hoe to slice off weeds, not to damage the sweetcorn's surface-growing roots. These can be protected by building up soil around the stems in mounds, which will also encourage further stabilizing roots to form, allowing the plants to cope better in stronger winds.

It is possible to undercrop between sweetcorn plants, where space is limited. Sweetcorn's relatively compact foliage will allow sufficient light to penetrate and smaller vegetables grown in between, such as dwarf beans, radishes or lettuce, will not be crowded out.

Each individual sweetcorn plant will produce one or two cobs. Watch the tassels at the ends of the cobs: the time for harvesting will have arrived when these turn brown. Double-test for ripeness by removing part of a husk and squeezing a kernel inside. If the juice from the kernel appears milky, then the cob is ready. To harvest a cob, twist it away from the plant. It is possible to freeze cobs for longer-term storage.

SWEET POTATOES

Sweet potatoes are native to Central and South America where the climate is warm for most of the time, and they are cultivated commercially in most southern states of the USA. It is possible, however, to grow some varieties in more northerly climes, as long as the temperature remains at 60°F (15°C) towards the end of the growing season. These tender vegetables are related to morning glory (genus *Ipomoea*). They grow on vines that cover the soil, setting roots as they go. There are also bush varieties,

and these have short vines and work better in areas where there is limited space.

Don't expect to grow sweet potatos from seed. It is necessary to obtain 'slips' from an established vine from a local nursery. A common science project for schoolchildren entails placing a sprouting sweet potato, suspended on toothpicks, in a glass of water. The vine grows out the top and the roots grow down into the water. The vines growing from the top are usually white before gradually turning green with leaves. It is therefore possible to grow your own slips from a sweet potato, but it is still easier to buy them, which will ensure that the plants are as disease-resistant as possible.

Plant the slips directly into the soil in early summer when the ground temperature reaches 70°F (21°C). First make a wide, raised ridge in the ground about 8in (20cm) high. Plant the slips 12–15in (30–38cm) apart in the highest part of the ridge. As mentioned before, sweet potatoes love the heat so it would be beneficial to use black plastic covering to keep the soil warm. Allow about 3–4ft (1m or so) between rows as the vines need plenty of space.

You won't have to worry about weeds, since the vines will choke out anything that grows in their way. Water regularly and fertilize with a 5-10-10 water-soluble fertilizer every three weeks once they have become established. Most sweet potatoes take 100–110 days from slip to harvestable vegetable. Water only sporadically during the last three to four weeks before harvest.

TOMATOES

Seeds may be started off indoors by sowing them in pots of compost, although an alternative is to purchase young tomato plants in late May/early June. Tomatoes are grown mostly in greenhouses, where the climate is uncertain, although a few varieties can be grown outdoors.

Tomatoes like a nice warm spot in full sun, and at least eight hours of sunlight a day, or they become spindly and produce little mature fruit. They must be sheltered from the wind, or they can be grown against a wall or fence. Keep well away from the potato crop. A well-drained, fertile soil is an essential growing medium, preferably one that has been manured for a previous crop, otherwise apply a general fertilizer about two weeks before planting. Never apply fresh manure just before planting.

Sow seeds from mid March to early April in shallow drills in seed trays. When seedlings reach the three-leaf stage, prick out, transferring them to larger containers and allowing 2–3in (5–7.5cm) between plants. Alternatively, plant the seedlings individually in 2–3-in diameter peat pots.

Another method is to sow two or three seeds directly into 2–3-in diameter peat pots or peat blocks, thinning out the seedlings when they are at the three-leaf stage.

When the plants are about 7–8in (17–20cm) high, whatever the sowing method used, and once all danger of frost has passed (late May/early June), harden off the plants and transplant them outdoors (purchased tomato plants can also be planted out at this time).

The plants should be set about 18in (45cm) apart, with a 4-ft (120-cm) plus stake provided for each plant if they are tall-growing or cordon varieties. As the plants grow, tie in the

stems to the stake at 8-in (20-cm) intervals. When the first fruits begin to form, the plant will produce side shoots in between the main stem and the leaf stems. If allowed to remain, they will grow and produce a mass of foliage but few tomatoes. Therefore, they should be removed by pinching them out with the fingers. Once each plant has developed four or five trusses, pinch out the growing tip to stop further vertical growth.

It is important to water tomatoes regularly but without letting the compost become waterlogged. Irregular watering often results in split fruit. The time from sowing to harvesting is about 20 weeks.

TURNIPS

Grow turnips outdoors in open ground, prefererably in light, humus-rich soil, avoiding potential dry areas. Also avoid acid soil, adding lime if required. The soil should preferably have been manured for a previous crop.

For an early crop, start sowing seeds in March in ½-in (1.2-cm) deep drills, with about 9in (22cm) between rows. Sow thinly and cover with soil. Making repeated small sowings every month until early July will ensure a longer season of fresh turnips than a single sowing. Thin out the seedlings so that they are about 5in (13cm) apart.

For the main storage crop, plant turnips in late June or early July, so that roots can develop in the warmer weather, late plantings being less susceptible to damage by turnip-root maggot.

VEGETABLE MARROWS, COURGETTES (ZUCCHINI) & SQUASHES

This method can also be used to produce courgettes (zucchini) and the various squashes.

In late April, sow seeds indoors in pots filled with seed compost. Sow two seeds on their edges in a 2–3-in (5–7.5-cm) pot, at a depth of ½in (1.2cm), removing the weaker seedling in due course. Harden off and plant out the seedlings from late May to early June, allowing 15–24in (38–60cm) between plants for bush varieties, 18in

(45cm) for climbing varieties, and 4ft (120cm) for trailing varieties. Pinch out the growing tips of trailing varieties when they reach 24in (60cm) long.

Alternatively, sow seed outdoors from late May to early June in a very sheltered site (light shade is tolerated) with a moisture-retentive, humus-rich soil. Sow two or three seeds on their edges at a depth of 1in (2.5cm), under cloches or glass jars, allowing 15–24in

ABOVE: Courgettes.

LEFT: Vegetable marrow.

89

(38–60cm) between plants for bush varieties, 18in (45cm) for climbing varieties and 4ft (120cm) for trailing varieties. Remove the weaker seedlings in due course. Pinch out the growing tips of trailing varieties when they reach 24in (60cm) long.

Failure of the fruits to form is common, especially in dull, damp summers, while planting in soil that is too rich may result in luxuriant foliage but few fruits.

ABOVE: Starburst squash.

LEFT: Pumpkins.

CHAPTER THREE
GROWING HERBS

Herbs are defined as any of the herbaceous plants valued for their flavour, fragrance or medicinal properties. Herbs are easy to grow, and impart a finer, fresher, more vibrant flavour to food than the dried alternatives, which quickly go stale if kept in the cupboard for too long. Be sure to choose the right herb for the right location; most enjoy a sunny spot, and only a few, such as angelica, sweet woodruff and sweet cicely, are better grown in partial shade. Most do not require a highly fertile soil, which tends to produce excessive foliage that is poor in flavour. In fact, herbs grow best when soils contain only adequate organic matter. In areas where winter

temperatures never drop very far below freezing, there is the opportunity to grow many of the shrubby Mediterranean aromatics, and rosemary, lavender, marjoram, artemisia and santolina, for example, will grow larger and more attractive with each passing year.

In fact, many herbs originated in Mediterranean lands and so appreciate free-draining soils. Drainage can be improved by adding grit to planting holes. Avoid overfeeding; simply place a dressing of manure or compost around the bases of the plants each autumn, and only add liquid fertilizer during

Annual herbs include basil, coriander (cilantro) and marjoram, while the perennials include mint (whose roots must be contained to avoid it running amok, but which can be grown in pots sunk into the soil), thyme, rosemary, lavender and sage. Chives, garlic, and the other members of the onion family, are perennial plants originally grown from seed but more often from bulbs. Some herbs fall into the biennial category, which means they flower and develop seeds in their second season, and include parsley and caraway.

the growing season if plants appear to be struggling.

Most herbs are tough, wild plants which will thrive when given the

OPPOSITE LEFT: Chives, the smallest member of the onion family, have a milder, subtler taste.

OPPOSITE RIGHT: Dill is excellent with fish.

ABOVE: Coriander (cilantro): add chopped leaves to Indian and Asian dishes, also the ground-up seeds for a spicier flavour.

RIGHT: Fresh-smelling lemon-scented thyme goes well in chicken dishes.

luxurious conditions of a garden. When planting culinary herbs, divide them into those that enjoy full sun, such as rosemary, thyme, sweet basil, French tarragon, sage and oregano, and those happier in partial shade, such as sorrel, mizuna, rocket, mustard, parsley and chervil.

Like all plants, herbs fall into two categories: annual and perennial. Annuals live for a single year, flowering and developing seeds from which the next generation will grow. Perennial plants last for many years, and deserve to be given a permanent position where they can flower every year.

Herbs may be grown among vegetables, in formal parterres or with flowers in beds or herbaceous borders. They can even be grown in pots on the patio, or in hanging baskets near to the back door, so that they are within easy reach of the kitchen, and where they smell great on a hot summer's day.

OPPOSITE: This is curly-leaf parsley, but there is also a flat-leaf variety.

ABOVE: Oregano: the herb is tastier when dried.

RIGHT: Rosemary is not only beautiful in a garden, but also has important culinary uses.

RIGHT: Mint, a useful companion plant to roses and may help to deter aphids.

BELOW: Chervil, a delicate herb, is one of the *fines herbes* of French cuisine.

OPPOSITE: Sage can be used in stuffings and for flavouring meats.

The most common of the traditional culinary herbs are:

Basil

Chives

Coriander (cilantro)

Dill

Marjoram

Mint

Oregano

Parsley

Rosemary

Sage

Summer savory

Thyme

Winter savory

Most herbs can be grown from seed and sown directly into the soil. For an early harvest, start the seeds off in shallow trays indoors in late winter, then transplant the seedlings out after all risk of frost has passed. Harvest the leaves when the plant has sufficient foliage. Don't pick too many at a time, which will weaken the plant. The flavour of the leaves are at their best just before the plant comes into flower. Most herbs also produce seeds that can be used for flavouring food, and these can be gathered once flowering is over and seed heads have formed.

97

CHAPTER FOUR

GROWING FRUIT

GROWING SOFT FRUITS

Seasonal soft fruits, such as strawberries and raspberries, are the true taste of summer, and to grow them in your own backyard, picking them straight from the plant as they ripen, is a real treat. Home-grown fruit does not come any fresher: flavour is more pronounced, hinting of the health benefits in store, and you save money at the same time.

Fruit trees, bushes and plants can be grown anywhere: in flower borders, in vegetable plots, even in containers on patios. Most fruit plants like a sunny, sheltered position in soil that remains moist without becoming waterlogged,

RIGHT: Strawberries can be grown through black polythene, which deters weeds from growing and competing with the plants. It also keeps soil moist and prevents soil from splashing onto the fruit.

OPPOSITE: Gooseberries are more popular in Britain than they are in the USA.

98

and which is not too alkaline (slightly acid to neutral soil of pH 6–7 is ideal).

If soil is sandy, or there is heavy clay, dig in plenty of well-rotted organic matter before planting, such as garden compost or blended farmyard manure. This improves the ability of thin soil to hold water and adds nutrients at the same time. It also opens up heavy soil so that roots can spread out and grow.

Fruit plants are extremely hardy and are able to tolerate a surprising amount of damage. Birds are not the only pests competing for the first crops, so protect them with netting, but be sure to keep it taut to avoid birds getting caught up in it. Choosing disease-resistant varieties will ensure a good crop.

The best time to buy and transplant is when plants are not growing. Do this in late autumn or early spring when the soil has some residual warmth: in most areas, from mid October–mid December and from late February–early April are the best times.

Be sure to get plants back into the ground within a few days, keeping roots moist at all times. Bushes can stay in their pots until you are ready to plant them, provided they are kept watered.

BLUEBERRIES

Where blueberries are concerned, the first thing to consider are the type you wish to plant. Be sure to pick the variety that fits your available space and climate zone, and always purchase bushes from a reputable supplier.

Like most fruits and vegetables, blueberries require several hours a day in full sun, and anything less will have an impact on yields. Blueberries grow best in a fairly acid soil or one with a pH of 4–4.5. You may need to add sulphur to get the pH into the desired range or alternatively grow in pots containing ericaceous compost, occasionally giving a high potash feed during the growing season..

The soil should be a loamy mix, with about 4–7 per cent organic matter.

Blueberries have shallow roots, making drainage all-important. If soil is clay or poorly drained, then raised beds are a sensible option, or soil can alternatively be built up around the plants. It is always a good idea to introduce compost into your soil preparation.

Blueberries, in general, are self-pollinating, but like most fruits the yield and quality of the fruit can be

increased by adding a pollinator bush. As for the number of bushes to plant, four or five are usually enough for an average family, and can easily be handled even in a raised garden bed. The spacing of plants will vary according to variety, but is usually 5 or 6ft (1.5 or 1.8m) for larger varieties. Low bush varieties will typically be spaced about 3ft (1m) apart.

Be sure to plant after all danger of frost has passed. Assuming the soil has already been prepared to suit, dig a hole slightly larger by a few inches than the root ball, placing the plant in the hole, then packing the soil firmly around it. To encourage runner development, cover a little of the bush stems with soil. Given only a modicum of care, blueberries have the potential to last for many years.

CURRANTS

Red-, black- and whitecurrants are full of antioxidants, vitamin C and minerals. The bushes or canes are very easy to look after, and they can tolerate degrees of sun and shade. The most commonly grown is the blackcurrant.

Plant out bare-rooted stock from October through to March. If a currant bush has already been established in a container, it can be planted out at any time of year, avoiding periods of continual frost or waterlogged soil conditions. Currants are quite accommodating and do well either in sun or in dappled shade, while good air

circulation will reduce the risk of fungal diseases. The soil must be well-drained though moist; always avoid dry planting areas. Dig in plenty of well-rotted manure.

Bare-rooted stock usually comes via mail order as plain stems and roots. On arrival, and before planting out, place roots in a bucket of water and leave for 12–24 hours. Dig a hole that fits the roots comfortably, without bending or breaking them. Place the roots in the hole and replace the soil. Ensure that the base of the stem is level with the soil surface after the soil has been firmed down. Water thoroughly. In the case of an established plant, dig a hole wide enough for the roots and to a depth allowing the soil mark on the stem to match the soil surface. Position the plant and fill in with soil. Water in thoroughly and scatter well-rotted manure around the plant. Leave a space of 5ft (1.5m) between bushes.

Prune white- and redcurrants to reveal an open centre to the bush, allowing light to come in and air to circulate; this also makes for more convenient picking. When the plant is established, cut away branches that are close to the soil, leaving 4in (10cm) of stem. Prune away other branches to an outward-facing bud, cutting back roughly two-thirds of their length. Allow the bush to grow into the required shape and space in subsequent years, cutting back leading shoots by 50 per cent to an upright bud.

Blackcurrants should be pruned differently: once established, prune down to stubby shoots or leave two buds above ground level on each branch. When the first growing season is over, prune down to one strong shoot at soil level. In subsequent years, prune blackcurrants in winter to the shape and size required, leaving the centre open for light and air, and cutting away any older two-year-old branches – identifiable by their grey colour – also any blackened stems. Blackcurrants produce fruit on older growth.

Keep bushes free from surrounding weeds, and remove the suckers of red- or whitecurrants as they appear. Keep plants moist during dry spells, but be aware that overwatering may cause the skins of the fruit to split. Each spring, scatter a new layer of manure around the roots.

Protect the plants with netting or fruit cages, as birds will eat both the fruit and the developing buds. Harvest when the fruit is still firm but ripe.

Remove the currants as bunches or strings, or pick individual currants if they are to be eaten straightaway. Most soft fruit freezes well.

Currants are extremely versatile used fresh, cooked in pies and tarts, in juices, jams (jellies), and in the exquisite blackcurrant Crème de cassis liqueur.

GOOSEBERRIES

Soil must be fertile, well-drained but moist in order for gooseberries to thrive. Plant out in the autumn, choosing a sunny, sheltered location, in the absence of which, shady, relatively cool conditions will be tolerated. Prepare the ground by forking it over and removing weeds and stones. Dig a planting hole suitable for the root growth, then fork in some well-rotted manure or compost, combined with granules or pellets of general-purpose fertilizer, in the base. Gooseberries are also suitable for container planting.

The size of the planting hole should be around three times the diameter of the roots but no deeper than the roots. Spread out the roots of bare-rooted gooseberries in the prepared planting hole, covering them with soil. Avoid air pockets by placing soil between and around the roots. Firm the soil down and water in. Gooseberry bushes should be spaced at just over 3ft (1m) apart, allowing access for picking; cordons can be spaced at between 14 and 18in (35 and 45cm). Keep well-watered until the plants are established; use a mulch of bark or compost around the plants.

To plant a gooseberry bush in a container, fill the base with a layer of stones to allow for drainage. A terracotta pot around 14in (35cm) deep is ideal. Cover the stones with compost, then lower the roots of the bush down so that the soil mark on the stem matches the rim of the pot. Water in, then firm down the soil. Use a liquid fertilizer once a week.

The first harvest should be ready in late May to early June: remove around half the crop, leaving room for the remaining fruit to grow large. This early

crop can be used for cooking. A few weeks after the initial harvest, further crops can be picked.

Net gooseberries when they are fruiting to prevent them from becoming food for the birds. Weight the netting at the edges to stop birds from getting underneath. You may find it necessary to keep the netting on throughout the winter when some birds, such as bullfinches, may well feed on the buds.

Pruned and trained gooseberries will produce the best crops. The aim of winter pruning should be to form a balanced branch structure, while at the same time keeping the centre of the bush open. Cut back leading shoots by a third, then prune back shoots pointing towards the centre of the bush. In summer, side shoots can be pruned back to five leaves to encourage fruiting spurs to develop.

Train single-stemmed cordons against walls or onto canes, tying the leading-shoot tip into the support. As with bushes, prune side shoots back to five leaves during the summer. When winter comes, shorten the main tip by a quarter, and shorten side shoots to three buds, encouraging the formation of new fruit spurs for the following year.

BACKYARD FARMING

Check leaves for signs of caterpillars and pick them off by hand. Alternatively, use an insecticide if there are too many to handle. Steady watering when the fruits are developing will produce the best results; erratic watering, or heavy watering after a dry period, may cause splitting and rotting of the fruit.

RASPBERRIES

It is an easy matter to establish and maintain a raspberry patch, and if a mix of different varieties are used, including some of the thornless types, a fruiting season from June right through to the first frosts of autumn can be achieved. It is easiest to buy raspberry canes from a supplier, such as a nursery or garden centre.

Plant out the bare-rooted canes in autumn. Choose a spot in full sun or part shade where there is well-drained soil, having prepared the site several weeks earlier by digging the ground over and incorporating well-rotted organic matter into the soil. Remove weeds and stones.

Dig a planting hole deep enough for the soil mark on the stems of the canes to remain at the same level as the ground when planted. Carefully spread out the roots, lower the plant into the hole, then fill in with soil, firming in to prevent air pockets. Water well. Allow around 14–18in (35–45cm) between canes.

Raspberry canes tend to lean sideways, resulting in damaged fruit if left unsupported. Use wire between fence posts or tree stakes placed 10ft (3m) apart, or in a small patch use single supports with the raspberries trained around them. The supports should be roughly 8ft (2.5m) in height. Prune canes above a bud when they are around 12in (30cm) tall.

Raspberries need plenty of water: keep plants damp throughout the summer, scattering fertilizer over the soil around the canes in spring. It is also a good idea to lay down mulch to help retain moisture levels.

The fruits will redden quickly. Pick them regularly when firm, pulling each raspberry away from its plug, which should be left intact as part of the plant. Once picked, refrigerate the fruit to prevent it from perishing. It should remain fresh for three to six days.

During the autumn, prune fruiting canes back to ground level. Using garden twine, tie in a group of the

newly-grown canes, choosing around seven or eight of the strongest which will fruit next year. Remove the older canes. During the winter, cut away ungainly top growth. For later, autumn-fruiting varieties, prune old canes and tie in the new in mid winter. Old canes that are unlikely to fruit again are recognizable by the peeling, greyish bark on stem and branch.

Canes which show signs of disease or infestation should be removed. It is also good practice to remove those that now block access to your rows of canes or are outside the patch itself. These will block light and air circulation necessary for growth if they are not removed.

RHUBARB

Contrary to popular belief, rhubarb is actually a vegetable; however, it is treated as though it were a soft fruit for culinary purposes. Cultivated for its delicious, pink stems, rhubarb is a very hardy, frost-resistant plant; in fact, it requires a period of frost in winter in order to produce the best stems. It is important to remember, however, that the leaves contain oxalic acid and are poisonous if consumed. It is only the stems that will be used.

Plant out crowns in late autumn to early winter, October being ideal for the purpose. Rhubarb can be grown in shady areas (potential frost pockets should be avoided) and ideally in positions of partial shade. Rhubarb thrives in slightly acid soils with a pH of between 6 and 6.8. Ground that is prone to waterlogging should be avoided at all cost, and will result in rotting crowns.

Rhubarb will develop an extensive root system, therefore it is worth the effort to dig over the soil four weeks before planting. Remove stones and mix in compost and organic matter. Space rhubarb crowns 3ft (1m) apart in rows 3ft apart. Plant the roots with the

crown bud 2in (5cm) below the surface of the soil. The hole for the crown must be dug extra large and composted manure should be mixed with the soil to be placed around the roots. Firm in the soil, keeping it loose over the buds. Water well.

Remove flowers when they appear in early spring, as blooming and seeding will slow down the growth of the stems, with energy being diverted into growing seeds. Fertilizing in the early spring will also increase the rhubarb harvest significantly.

Once the leaves have died back, put down compost around the plants. There are few diseases to watch out for during the year, and as long as the soil is well-drained, the crowns should not succumb to rot. You will notice, if they do, that a fungus at the base of the stems is causing them to turn brown and soft. Remove the plant and destroy it straight away.

Established rhubarb plants need to be divided or split into three or four separate crowns roughly every five years. This should be done during winter dormancy, using a spade. When doing this, ensure that each new crown has a bud that will shoot during the coming growing season.

STRAWBERRIES

Three types of strawberries are commonly grown: June-bearing, Everbearing, and Day Neutral, the most popular being the June-bearing. Strawberries grow very well in containers, which is useful if space is at a premium, and they are ideal for growing in raised beds.

Strawberries thrive in well-drained soil in full sun or part shade. It is easiest to grow strawberries from plants bought from a nursery or garden centre. The best time to plant them is in early autumn or spring. If planting in spring, remove any flower buds so that the plant's energy is concentrated on developing roots and becoming established. Space the plants 16in (40cm) apart in rows 3ft (1m) apart. Water well. It is a good idea to mulch the plants with a thick layer of well-rotted manure, compost or straw (some

gardeners grow their plants through black polythene). This impenetrable layer will prevent weeds from growing and competing with the plants. It will also keep the soil moist, cutting down on watering.

Flowering starts from early summer onwards, and the fruit will develop from the flowers as they die down. The young fruits now need to be protected from mud damage, and it is an easy matter to mulch with straw or tuck handfuls of straw under the fruit trusses to ensure they are not in direct contact with the soil. Once the fruits have ripened (when they are deep red in colour and slightly soft to the touch), simply pick them gently off the plant.

After the final fruits have been harvested, cut the remaining foliage down to about 4in (10cm) above the crown to allow new leaves to grow. Clear away and burn any debris from around the plants (including removed foliage). This prevents disease from building up around the plants and hampering growth the following year. Water the plants thoroughly and apply a mulch of well-rotted manure or garden compost to add nutrients to the soil. You will notice, at the end of the fruiting season, that the plants will

have developed several runners, with small plants growing from them. These grow roots and can become new plants. In late summer, simply insert the individual plantlets attached to the runners into small pots filled with cutting compost. Sever each young plant from its parent once it has rooted.

GROWING FRUIT

Growing and Maintaining Fruit
Trees
One or two fruit trees should be enough
to produce abundant fruit for most
needs, given that there is sufficient space
in your backyard, while showers of pink
or white blossom will gladden the eye in
spring. Fruit trees come in all shapes
and sizes and so do their roots, which
means you can choose exactly the right
type for your plot – whether it be a giant
tree or one that can be grown in a pot.

APPLES

Apple trees are likely to yield fruit for over 40 years, and a productive tree will provide a store of apples to last right through until spring. They are usually bought as bare-rooted stock, or you could try growing them from seed if time is on your side. Many believe apples need plenty of room, but they can be accommodated in whatever space is available, be they full-sized trees, bushes, cordons, espaliers trained along walls and fences, or those grown in containers as patio plants. Many apple cultivars are currently available. When making a selection, consider fruit size, taste, colour, blossom period, ripening season, disease-resistance and pollen compatibility, all of which are important factors.

Apple trees are ideally planted between October and December. A position in full sun is desirable, although some shade can be tolerated. The soil should be relatively free-draining, and areas that tend to become waterlogged or which are subject to frost, likely to kill off the blossom, should be avoided at all cost. The type of soil is not crucial, and a medium soil that is slightly acid with moderate

wide, then mix in plenty of well-rotted organic material. Remember that the soil needs to be at a medium level of fertility, otherwise the tree will take on too much growth but produce very little fruit. If the planting location is in the centre of a lawn, also mix into the planting hole a long-lasting fertilizer such as bonemeal. Position the tree in the hole and fill in with soil, ensuring that the noticeable 'grafting joint', between the rootstock and the scion (the trunk above the joint), is above the level of the soil by 2in (5cm) or more. Use your feet to firm down the soil and water in thoroughly. Some

fertility would suffice, though extremes of acidity and alkalinity are best avoided.

In general, the advice is to plant two trees to ensure pollination, but in a reasonably populated area a single apple tree is likely to be pollinated by neighbouring trees as bees move from one to another over a wide area. It is probably best to start off with a young tree from a nursery, which will produce apples that much sooner. To plant a bare-rooted tree, prepare the soil around one month ahead. Dig a hole 20–24in (50–60cm) deep and 3ft (1m)

varieties will need support, in which case stakes should be placed 3–4in (8–10cm) away and the tree tied to them. Use plastic rather than metal ties, which will not damage the tree. Check them as the tree grows and readjust as necessary to avoid ties cutting into the trunk.

To train a tree to grow along a fence or wall, choose a south-facing location and ensure that the supporting structure will not collapse under the weight of fruit. A framework of trellis or horizontal wires will permit the branches to be trained into position, while also allowing the tree itself to support much of its own weight. The spacing of wires in the framework should match the distance between the branches or 'arms' of the tree, i.e., around 14–25in (35–50cm) apart. Plant out as above, digging the planting hole out from the side of the wall or fence.

Apples which twist off easily from the tree are likely to be ripe, or you could try one and see. Different varieties fruit at different times, but the season can be prolonged by planting out a selection of varieties which will provide a staggered crop. Take care not to damage or knock apples when harvesting them as they bruise

relatively easily, and bruises encourage rot. The sunnier the position of the tree, the more time will be available for the fruit to ripen. Fruit that ripens later in the season will tend to be more suitable for winter storage. Keep apples in a cool, dark, well-ventilated store such as a shed or garage.

Pruning the trees is vital. Pruning at different times of the year produces different effects. Winter pruning during the tree's period of dormancy triggers greater growth in the forthcoming season; summer pruning causes growth to slow down; spring pruning produces a combined effect.

In the case of a one-year-old bare-rooted tree, cut off the top half of the trunk with a pair of secateurs soon after planting. A two-, three- or four-year-old tree should have its black side shoots pruned by one-third between December and February; pink growth from the previous year should be left untouched and only cut away if it has become diseased. Prune above an outward-facing bud. Five-year-old trees are by now mature, having established their shape; prune them to keep the centre clear, removing growth that is weak or diseased. Try to maintain an equal balance between growth

produced in the last year, on which apples will grow, and older growth. Cordons need to be pruned in August, with side shoots pruned back to three leaves. Tie down new growth to keep a trained tree growing sideways.

To deter overwintering pests, use a horticultural, oil-based winter wash in December or January. A lighter

summer oil may be used during the growing season, and a grease band placed at 20in (50cm) above soil level will protect the tree from moths, the caterpillars of which eat leaves and fruit. Thin out fruit before harvest time; removing small or misshapen apples will give the good apples more of a chance to fill out.

CHERRIES

Plant trees at any time between late autumn and early winter when they are dormant, avoiding periods of frost. Choose a site with well-drained, fairly light soil. Soil pH should be between 6 and 7. You can check how well a particular site is draining by digging a planting hole; if rainwater remains in the hole over several days, then waterlogging is a problem. Frost pockets should also be avoided. Cherry trees are not as frequently grown as apples, therefore a pair of trees will be required if your chosen variety is not self-fertilizing.

Dig over the site a few weeks in advance of planting, removing weeds and stones. Before planting the trees,

soak the roots. Then use a spade to dig a hole which needs to be at least a third wider than the roots, though no deeper; fork over the soil at the bottom of the hole. Stake out by placing a stake next to the root before filling in the hole with soil, mounding it towards the base of the tree. Firm the soil down gently with your feet and water in thoroughly. Keep the tree watered until it is well-established, feeding regularly.

Alternatively, half-fill a container or pot with soil-based potting compost, plant the tree, and fill up with more compost. If planting to grow against a wall, plant the tree around 6–8in (15–20cm) away from it. A sunny location is usually required, but there are some dwarf varieties that can be grown on north-facing walls.

Harvest cherries between early June and the end of July, depending on the weather. Pick the cherries with their stalks intact. If, in the run-up to the harvest, the days are rather grey, use a silver-lined reflective material, available from specialist nurseries and garden centres. This is laid on the ground so that light is reflected back up onto the fruit, but laying down pebbles or flints around the base of the tree can achieve much the same purpose.

a growing node. Sap will then build up at this point and a bud will grow. Make the score horizontally into the bark across the trunk.

Use netting to keep birds away. Netting a dwarf cherry tree is relatively easy but a full-sized tree can be rather more difficult. It is possible to net individual clusters, or use whatever bird-scaring method that is most effective. To deter aphids, plant wild flowers around trees to encourage aphid-eating ladybirds (ladybugs) and lacewings to visit.

Pruning is essential. Bushes and trees may be pruned from year two onwards to produce a conical shape with branches shortening towards the top. In April, once the tree is in leaf, cut growth back to a bud or side shoot, cutting the bush back into its ideal conical shape in August. This shape allows light to reach all parts of the tree, and most crucially to the trunk from which new branches will grow. Branches which have borne a crop of fruit for five to six years will begin to weaken, and will need to be cut away. Don't prune cherry trees in winter. Be aware that fruit buds grow on branches which are two or more years old.

To encourage or trigger the growth of a new branch, use a pruning saw to gently score or 'notch' the trunk above

PEACHES & NECTARINES

Peaches have been grown in Asia for more than 2,000 years, produced for centuries in the United States, and thrive on a commercial basis in Mediterranean areas. Peaches are regarded as the 'queen' of fruits, coming second only to apples in popularity because of their food value and fine flavour. Nectarines can be used in the same way as peaches: genetically, the only difference between the two is the absence of fuzz on the nectarine's skin. Usually, nectarines are smaller than peaches, with both red and yellow colouring in the skin and a rather more pronounced aroma.

Both require sunny sites and protection from frost when in blossom. For these reasons they are unsuitable for areas prone to hard frosts. Therefore, the growing of free-standing trees in cooler areas, such as the UK and parts of North America, is not recommended. In cooler climes, however, when grown as fan-trained trees against south-facing walls, large crops of delicious fruit will be produced.

Correct positioning and soil type are the keys to growing peaches and nectarines successfully. Both produce

blossom in early spring which, if damaged by frost, will never go on to produce fruit. For this reason a south-facing wall (house walls are ideal), protected from wind, is the only satisfactory site. A fully-grown fan peach tree will have a spread of approximately 16ft (5m) and a height of 8ft (2.5m), so walls need to be large enough to accommodate this growth. Also bear in mind that wire supports will need to be nailed to the wall so that branches can be trained along their length.

Soil must be pre-dug (August is the ideal time) to a depth of 2ft 6in (75cm) a couple of months before planting to allow it to settle. Plenty of compost should be added to make the soil capable of holding water, but at the same time allow the excess to drain away. The soil should be neither too acid nor too alkaline.

Dig a planting hole 6ft (1.8m) x 3ft (1m) to a depth of 2ft 6in (75cm), adding garden compost and/or other organic matter. Scatter two or three handfuls of bonemeal or other long-lasting fertilizer into the hole and dig it in well. Plant the tree, then attach it to the pre-prepared wire frame, training the branches of the tree along the wires as it grows.

PEARS

Pear trees are widely cultivated across the world, the fruit being juicier than apples and generally softer in texture. The pear belongs in the same plant family as the apple, and bears similar flowers. Being deep-rooted trees, pears prefer a light loamy soil avoiding extremes of pH. The planting site must be sheltered from strong winds, avoiding locations where frost pockets occur. It is more difficult to establish a pear tree in a given location if the soil is allowed to dry out.

Factors to consider are the size of the tree (usually between 10 and 20ft/ 3 and 6m high), the variety and taste of the fruit, and ease of pollination. Varieties such as Conference are self-fertile, otherwise a pair of trees must be planted to ensure fertilization. But a single tree in a neighbourhood where there are many backyards, is quite likely to be pollinated by adjacent trees, but cannot always be guaranteed.

Plant bare-rooted trees between December and early March, when they are in their period of dormancy, but ready-grown, potted trees can be planted out at any time of the year. To plant a bare-rooted tree, prepare the

soil a month ahead. Dig a hole a little wider and deeper than the roots of the young tree. Mix in plenty of well-rotted organic material, bearing in mind that the soil needs to be at a medium level of fertility. If the chosen location is in the middle of a lawn, mix in a long-lasting fertilizer such as bonemeal. Place the tree in position and fill in with soil, ensuring that the noticeable grafting joint, between the rootstock and the scion (the trunk above the joint) stands proud of the soil level by 2in (5cm) or more. Firm down the soil with your feet and water in thoroughly. Some varieties will need staking out, in which case use the same method as described in the section on Apples.

If the intention is to train a tree to grow along a supporting fence or wall, choose a south-facing location and ensure that the supporting structure is strong enough to bear the weight of fruit. A framework of horizontal wires will allow the tree to be trained into position while also allowing it to support much of its own weight. The spacing of the wires in the framework should match the distance between the branches or 'arms' of the tree, being around 14–20in (35–50cm) apart. Plant

out as above, digging the planting hole out from the side of the wall or fence.

Pear trees tend to drop fruit in early to mid June; don't be alarmed, this is a natural occurrence. A month later, thin the fruit out further to allow the remaining pears to reach a good size. As a rough guide, pears can be thinned to leave around 3–5in (8–12cm) between fruit on the tree.

Depending on the rootstock, a pear tree will produce fruit after 3–5 years and a productive lifespan of up to 200 years may be expected according to variety.

Prune during winter, when the trees are dormant, opening a space in the centre to allow light in and air to circulate. The shape of a tree is formed by pruning over the first eight years,

allowing eight main fruiting branches to develop. Be gentle, as branches are relatively fragile compared with those of apple trees. Keep an equal balance between older growth and last season's growth. Cordons need to be pruned in August, with side shoots pruned back to three leaves. Tie down new growth to keep a trained tree growing sideways. Pests can be deterred in the same way as for apples (see Apples section above). Expose and kill pear midges when they are still on the ground by raking over the soil surface from late January through to late March, which is also the time when mulch can be spread around trees so that water is retained in the soil. If using compost as a mulch, leave a free space around the trunk.

Pears for storage should be harvested when still firm. They damage easily, so check them thoroughly for bruises. They don't benefit from being wrapped, so arrange them in a single layer on slatted shelves or in storage trays. Store for a few weeks only, after which they will need to finish off the ripening process. A week before you are ready to eat them, move the pears into a warm spot to ripen up, and eat within a few days.

PLUMS

October or November are the optimum months for planting out plum trees, but this is also possible, though more risky, from late autumn through to early spring. Plums require warmth and plenty of light, so a moist spot in full sun would be ideal. Avoid frost pockets, and you would be well-advised to choose a late-flowering variety in cooler areas. A good draining soil is important, and remember to plant a pair of trees rather than one if it is not self-pollinating.

If space is at a premium, choose a half-size or small variety which can be trained against a wall. First soak the roots, then use a spade to dig a hole. This needs to be at least a third wider than the roots, though no deeper; fork over the soil at the bottom of the hole. Stake the tree out, placing the stake next to the root before filling in the hole with soil, mounding it towards the base of the tree. Keep the grafted part of the tree at least 2in (5cm) above the level of the soil. Firm the soil down gently with your feet, and water in thoroughly. Keep the tree watered until it is established, feeding regularly. If growing against a wall, plant around

6–8in (15–20cm) away. Water plum trees thoroughly, avoiding waterlogging. In early spring, spread compost around the tree to a depth of up to 6in (15cm).

Plum trees won't produce fruit until year four or five, and harvesting lasts for around four weeks. Thin plums out to relieve stress on branches and to concentrate flavour and energy

in smaller, higher-quality crops. Pick plums once they are easily removable, and discard any that are damaged and which will attract wasps and disease. Hang up 'wasp traps' (jars filled with

sugary water) to prevent the theft of your fruit.

Prune when the fruiting period has ended. Cut away old, dead branches, maintaining the tree's shape, be it fan-trained against a wall, free-standing in a pyramid, a bush or standard tree. Pruning will also help to control silver leaf disease. Pull out mini-trees or 'suckers', which grow up from the roots. Don't prune when trees are dormant in winter. To deter overwintering pests, a horticultural oil-based winter wash can be applied in December or January. During the growing season, a lighter summer oil can be used, and protect from moths by applying a grease band 20in (50cm) above soil level.

Ripe plums are highly perishable but will last for a few days stored in a fridge. Under-ripe plums will ripen slowly if stored in a paper-lined box in a dark, cool environment.

CHAPTER FIVE

DISEASES, PESTS & BENEFICIAL INSECTS

Both vegetables and fruit can suffer attack from diseases and pests. Use organic controls where possible, otherwise use chemicals, but wisely.

DAMPING-OFF A fungal infection that commonly affects seedlings, causing them to rot at soil level and keel over. It is usually encouraged by a combination of any, or all, of the following conditions: crowding seedlings, overwatering, poor air circulation, dirty containers and contaminated soil or water. Always sow seeds thinly in fresh, sterilized compost in clean pots. Water sparingly with fresh tap water, preferably using Cheshunt compound or some other copper-based fungicide, such as Bordeaux mixture.

SOOTY MOULD A black fungus that grows on aphid honeydew deposited on plants. Remove by hosing plant down, or use soapy water to wipe leaves.

DISEASES OF VEGETABLES
ANTHRACNOSE This fungal disease most commonly affects squashes, legumes, peppers, sweetcorn, and tomatoes. It appears on leaves as irregular yellow, brown, dark-brown or black spots, also as circular lesions on vegetables which soon become sunken and gradually turn black. Spray plants with Bordeaux mixture, stopping when the first flowers appear. The disease is seed-borne, so destroy plants after cropping and avoid growing beans in the same position for a couple of years.

BLACK ROT A disease found on stored roots, which shows itself as black sunken patches near to the necks. There is no known control and the infected roots should be destroyed.

BLOSSOM END ROT A serious disorder of tomatoes, peppers, and aubergines (eggplants), in which a dry, sunken area of decay develops on the blossom end (opposite the stem) of the fruit, especially the first of the season. This is a physiological disorder related to calcium deficiency. Regular and even watering helps to prevent the problem arising.

BORON DEFICIENCY An uncommon disorder affecting plants growing in deficient soils and associated with areas of high rainfall and leached soils. Boron may be present but locked up in soils with a high pH, and the deficiency may be worse in wet seasons. Commonly called crown or heart rot, in which the central leaves die and become black; roots may also turn black inside. Ensure that the ground has plenty of organic matter incorporated and that a liquid seaweed feed or fertilizer is given.

CELERY LEAF SPOT Brown spots appear on leaves, developing into black pustules. Most purchased seed is treated against this virus but self-saved seed may succumb to it. Spray every fortnight with Bordeaux mixure, until just before harvesting.

CHOCOLATE SPOT Affects broad beans (fava beans) and appears as brown spots on leaves. In severe cases the stems turn black. Spray with Bordeaux mixture.

CLUB ROOT A devastating disease affecting brassicas, and including swedes (rutabaga) and radishes. It is a soil-borne fungus that causes roots to thicken and distort, the effect being worse on badly-drained and acid soils. It survives in the soil indefinitely and can be transmitted via soil stuck to boots, which is transferred to other parts of the plot. There is no cure, but various methods can be used to reduce its effects.

CROWN GALL A bacterial infection associated with badly-drained soils that causes lumps to appear on the sides of root crops. Rectify drainage problems before replanting.

CUCUMBER MOSAIC VIRUS Attacks all members of the squash family, causing leaves to turn yellow and pucker and growth to be stunted. There is no cure, therefore all affected plants must be destroyed. Control aphids that carry the disease.

FOOT & ROOT ROT The fungi causing this affect a wide variety of plants, including trees and vegetables, in which rot at the base of the plant spreads up the main stem, causing discolouring as it progresses, and often making the plant collapse completely. Normally introduced by an already-infected plant, but can be brought in on garden implements and machinery. Once in the soil, spores can overwinter for several years. Very difficult, if not impossible to remove icompletely.

GANGRENE A fungal disease of stored potatoes, causing them to rot. Only damaged or wet potatoes are likely to be affected. Ensure that only dry, undamaged potatoes are put into store.

HALO BLIGHT Bacterial infection in which brown spots appear on leaves, surrounded by a lighter halo. As this is seed-borne, and usually treated by seedsmen, it is not very common and will only appear if using your own saved seeds.

LEAF ROLL Affects tomatoes, and may be caused by environmental stresses, such as excess moisture or nitrogen and transplant shock. May also be related to moisture conservation during periods of extreme heat and drought. Avoid overwatering and irrigate during periods of dry weather. Make sure plants are properly hardened off before transplanting ouside. Avoid severe pruning of staking varieties and minimize damage if cultivating around roots. Plant growth and fruit production will be unaffected if the problem is recognized early enough and action taken.

MAGNESIUM DEFICIENCY Magnesium is one of the major constituents of chlorophyll. Signs are a paling of the leaves between veins which eventually turn brown and die. Most often occurs in very acid or very alkaline soils. Check pH and rectify. An application of Epsom salts, applied at a strength of 2oz per gallon of water and sprayed on the foliage at fortnightly intervals, may also help.

DISEASES, PESTS & BENEFICIAL INSECTS

MANGANESE DEFICIENCY
Indicated by yellowing between the veins of older leaves. Leaf-edges may become slightly in-curled and brown. Many types of plant may be affected from time to time. Very sandy and very alkaline soils may be deficient in manganese. In severe cases apply a foliar feed of manganese sulphate at a dilution of 2oz per 5 gallons of water.

MOSAIC VIRUS or YELLOW VIRUS
Also known as spinach blight, the virus affects the leaves by turning them yellow. There is no cure and affected plants should be destroyed.

NECK ROT A serious disease of onions, causing them to rot in store, the fungus having entered the bulb during its period of growth. It is much worse in wet years and in cases where the onion plants have been grown too strongly with too much manure or fertilizer. Heavy feeding also leads to 'thick-neck' onions, which do not store well. Destroy all rotted onions – they are a source of infection for the following year. Dress seeds and sets with a dusting of a systemic fungicide before sowing. To help eradicate spores, do not replant for two years.

PARSNIP CANKER The disease causes brown marks to appear around the neck of the root. Use only resistant varieties.

POTATO BLACKLEG A bacterial disease affecting the stems of infected plants, turning them black and rotten. Plants are stunted, wilted, and eventually die. Remove and burn infected plants and tubers. Only plant certified tubers.

POTATO BLIGHT First shows itself as black or brown blotches on the leaves. In more severe cases the plants turn yellow and eventually die. Affected tubers will rot and should not be stored. Treat by spraying the whole crop with a copper-based fungicide such as Bordeaux mixture.

RUST Attacks leeks, beans, beetroot (beets) and spinach and shows itself as bright-orange pustules on the leaves. Cool temperatures and high humidity favours rust. Sulphur and other fungicides, applied when rust first occurs, are helpful in control. Resistant varieties may be available.

SCAB Causes ugly marks on potato tubers. Avoid by incorporating plenty of organic matter into the soil and watering well during dry weather. Use resistant varieties of potatoes.

SCLEROTINA ROT This occurs when carrots are incorrectly stored, causing a white, fluffy mould to grow on or near the neck of the root. Black spores develop, infecting other roots. Ensure that there is plenty of ventilation and that only sound roots are stored. Remove and destroy any roots so infected.

SOFT ROT A bacterial disease affecting turnips and swedes with a grey or white mushy rot. Worse on badly-drained soil. To prevent, rotate crops and increase drainage.

SPRAING Causes red or brown marks to appear on the flesh of potatoes. There is no cure, but some potato varieties are resistant.

TOMATO LEAF MOULD The tops of the leaves turn yellow and purplish brown patches appear on the undersides. Prevent by encouraging good airflow around plants. Remove any infected leaves and spray with a fungicide.

VERTICILLIUM WILT More usual on tomatoes, the plants wither in hot weather but pick up at night. Leaves turn yellow and brown streaks run through the stems. Spray plants and soil with a fungicide and mulch around the stems so that new roots can form. Avoid growing tomatoes in the same soil for at least two years.

VIOLET ROOT ROT A serious, soil-borne fungal disease, causing wilting of the plant and yellowing of the leaves. When lifted, the roots have a web of purple threads around them. It particularly affects beets, parsnips, carrots, asparagus and potatoes. There is no cure and infected crops should be dug up and destroyed. Do not replant with any susceptible crops for a period of three years.

WHITE ROT Shows itself as a mouldy growth near to the necks of onions, which then rot. Remove bulbs and do not store. Spraying with a fungicide may help if the condition is caught early enough.

DISEASES OF FRUIT
AMERICAN MILDEW A powdery, white coating appears on the new shoots of gooseberries, spreading to young leaves and eventually the fruit. The gooseberries are small and may be covered in what resembles brown felt. Spray with a fungicide at the first signs and then at fortnightly intervals. Ensure that the bush is kept well-pruned and the centre of the bush open. (See also Powdery Mildew)

APPLE CANKER A common fungal disease of apple and pear trees, causing disfiguring, sunken patches of dead bark on fruiting spurs and branches. The infection may girdle the stem, killing it in a single season. Infected branches should be cut out and burned. Spray with Bordeaux mixture once after picking but before leaf fall and a second time when about half the leaves have fallen.

APPLE SCAB Apple scab and pear scab are two fungal diseases that cause dark, scabby marks on fruit and leaves. They are so similar that they are dealt with in the same way. Fungicides give good control when used according to manufacturers' schedules. For the

most effective control, the entire tree must be treated, but this is easier said than done.

BACTERIAL CANKER Particularly affects the stems and leaves of plums and cherries, but also apricots, peaches and ornamental Prunus species, causing sunken patches on bark and small 'shotholes' in leaves, often accompanied by a gummy ooze. Cut out all cankered areas, pruning back to healthy wood and applying a wound paint to protect from re-infection. Burn prunings. Alternatively, cut out infected areas and spray with a copper fungicide from mid summer to autumn at fortnightly intervals.

BITTER PIT A disease of apples, caused by chemical imbalance in the tree, this being either a shortage of calcium or too much potassium or magnesium. Often caused by shortage of water at a crucial time in the development of the apples. The condition causes brown sunken patches on the skins, which usually shows up on stored apples. There is no real treatment, but mulch (not straw) around the tree the following season, using well-rotted compost to conserve water, especially in dry periods. Do not over-fertilize.

BLACKCURRANT RUST Causes yellow patches on the undersides of the leaves in early summer. Spray with Dithane immediately after harvest.

BLOSSOM WILT A fungal disease of apples, pears, plums, cherries and related ornamental trees, which kills blossoms, spurs and small branches. The problem is caused by the same fungi responsible for brown rot in fruit.

BORON DEFICIENCY (see under DISEASES OF VEGETABLES)

BROWN ROT A fungal disease of apples, pears, plums, cherries and other fruit and ornamental trees, causing a brown, spreading rot in the fruit. Caused by the same fungi responsible for blossom wilt of the flowers and fruit spurs. No chemical treatment, but carry-over of the pathogens can be reduced by removing all rotted fruit promptly and composting them. Infection is via wounds, especially those caused by birds, so net trees to reduce bird damage if possible. Prune out and burn infected spurs and blossoms to

reduce the amount of fungus available to infect the fruit.

CANE BLIGHT A fungal infection that attacks raspberries, manifesting itself as a sudden wilting of the cane or foliage. The spores can live for up to four years on dead tissue, so cut out infected stems and burn. Do not compost. Fortunately, even badly-affected plants can recover the following year.

CANE SPOT Attacks raspberries, showing itself as small purple spots which spread and split. Cut out affected canes and treat with a fungicide.

CORAL SPOT A fungus that can affect all woody plants, including fruit trees and some soft fruits, and appears as small, pinkish-red, cushion-like pustules on branches of trees and on shrubs. It infects by penetrating wounds or pruning cuts. Cut out and burn any infected branches.

DIEBACK A fungal infection attacking gooseberries, in which the plant begins to die from the tips of its leaves backwards along stems. Remove affected stems, treating cuts with

Arbrex. Spray the whole plant with a fungicide.

FIREBLIGHT A serious disease increasingly found in pears and related trees. The disease enters through blossoms and rapidly spreads to the rest of the tree. The leaves remain attached and the tree looks as if it has been burnt. Treatment involves cutting out infected branches, or in serious cases removing the tree itself.

FOOT & ROOT ROT (see under DISEASES OF VEGETABLES)

GREY MOULD (BOTRYTIS) This fluffy mould affects most soft fruit and is more prevalent during wet summers. Remove any plant material that is affected and ensure that the plants are sprayed with a fungicide as a precaution.

HONEY FUNGUS Also known as white rot, this can affect all woody plants and trees. Recognizable by the presence of cream-coloured mycelium, smelling strongly of mushrooms, beneath the bark at the base of the trunk or stem, sometimes extending upwards, with a gum or resin exuding from cracks in the bark. Cream/honey-coloured mushrooms can be found growing around the base of the infected plant, usually in autumn. Dark or black root-like strands (rhizomorphs), often referred to as 'bootlaces', also appear beneath the bark and around the roots. Dig out and destroy infected plants. Do not replant with woody species on the same site for at least one year and choose trees/shrubs which are resistant when replanting.

LEAF MOULD The top surfaces of the leaves of fruit trees become yellow and the undersides brown. Most modern varieties of fruit are resistant to the disease, but if older varieties are affected, spray with a copper fungicide.

LEAF SCORCH Can be caused by many adverse environmental conditions, including soil compaction, transplant shock, nutrient deficiency, drought, salt toxicity and injury from herbicides. The loss of leaves is seldom immediately fatal, but conditions causing them must be corrected to avoid the decline or death of the tree or shrub. Plants under stress are also subject to attack by insects or diseases. To help prevent leaf scorch, prune out sprouts and diseased areas, and

maintain vigour through correct watering and fertilizing.

LEAF SPOT A disease affecting blackcurrants and gooseberries. Brown spots appear on the leaves which then drop off. This weakens the plant and the crop is reduced the following year. Spray with a fungicide at fortnightly intervals. Ensure that dropped leaves are removed and burnt.

MAGNESIUM DEFICIENCY (see under DISEASES OF VEGETABLES)

PEACH LEAF CURL Affects peaches, nectarines and almonds and causes red blisters to appear on the leaves, which eventually turn black and fall off. It is important to treat early, using a copper-based fungicide. Treat in late winter and again two weeks later, then again in autumn. Another way is to protect trees from rain between January and late May, which prevents fungal spores from touching the plant.

PEAR SCAB (see APPLE SCAB)

PEAR STONEY PIT A viral disease of pears. The fruit is small and misshapen, the skin covered in small

craters and lumps. It is more common where very old trees are concerned. There is no cure and the tree must be uprooted and burned.

POWDERY MILDEW A fungal disease affecting a wide range of plants. It is one of the easier to spot, its symptoms being quite distinctive, with infected plants displaying white, powdery spots on leaves and stems. The lower leaves are the most affected, but the mildew can appear on any above-ground part of the plant. Chemical control is possible with fungicides, but growing cultivars resistant to the disease may be a better method of control.

REVERSION This viral disease, found mostly on blackcurrants, causes changes in leaf shape and the leaf buds to become red. It is spread by the Big Bud Mite (see also under PESTS) and, once infected, the plants begin slowly to decline. There is no cure and affected plants must be dug up and burnt.

RUSSETING This is normal on a few varieties of apple and is how they get their name, but it sometimes occurs on varieties that it shouldn't and leads to unsightly fruit. The eating quality is not

DISEASES, PESTS & BENEFICIAL INSECTS

affected and the cause can be put down to poor growing weather.

SHOTHOLE DISEASE
A fungal disease affecting plums, peaches and cherries, and which causes small holes to appear in the leaves. Only weak trees are affected and it should not occur if the tree is well-fed.

SILVER LEAF
This is a serious disease of plum trees, but can also affect apples, cherries and peaches, in which leaves take on a silver sheen, turn brown, then drop of. Dieback of shoots also occurs and when the wood is cut into, a black ring can be seen. Cut out all dead branches below the level of infection and paint all wounds with Arbrex. In severe cases, toadstools may appear at the base of the tree, in which case the tree must be dug out and burnt.

SILVER LEAF (FALSE)
Resembles silver leaf at first glance, but the cut wood will not display the distinctive black ring. This is caused by a lack of water, and can be remedied by putting down a thick mulch in spring and watering well.

SPUR BLIGHT
Purple patches appear around the buds on raspberries and loganberries, turn silver, and the buds die. Cut out and burn infected canes and spray with fungicide.

STRAWBERRY MILDEW
A common disease of strawberries causing dark patches to appear on the upper surfaces of leaves with a silvery-grey mould on the undersides. The fruit can also be affected. Spray with a fungicide as directed by the manufacturer. Remove and burn all foliage after harvesting.

VIRUSES
Viruses usually show themselves in the form of a yellowing mottling of the leaves. There is no cure. Prevent infection by controlling the aphids that carry the virus. In mild cases, cut out infected parts or branches and destroy by burning.

PESTS
APHIDS
These may be green, yellow, brown, red or black, depending on the species and the plants on which they feed. A few species appear waxy or woolly, due to the secretion of a waxy white or grey substance over their body surface. Aphids sap plants with devastating effects, depositing a sticky honeydew to which disease spores can attach themselves, so causing further problems. They can also spread virus diseases. Tackle the problem as soon as it is identified, either by squashing the aphids by hand or spraying if they are too numerous. Because each adult aphid can produce up to 80 offspring in a matter of a week, populations have the potential of increasing with great rapidity.

APPLE SAWFLY
Small wasp-like insects which lay their eggs on the blossom. The eggs then grow into maggots which tunnel under the surface of the skin of the fruit, which causes scars on the outside . As the maggots grow, they tunnel into the middle of the fruit, causing it to drop prematurely. Preventative treatment consists of spraying with derris when most of the

apple blossom has fallen from the tree. Destroy affected fruit by burning.

BEAN FLY The flies lay their eggs in the bean leaf tissue. The maggots which hatch from these eggs then mine into the leaf tissue and tunnel down the leaf stalks, finally making their way down into the stem. There they feed and destroy the inner tissues of the stems, causing the plants to wilt and finally fall over and die. This is devasting, but sowing seeds indoors and planting out will lessen its effect.

BEET CARRION BEETLE The grub and adult of this black beetle feed on the leaves of beetroots (beets) in spring. Spray with derris as soon as identified.

BEET-LEAF MINER The first signs are large, light-brown blisters on the leaves of beetroots, caused by the maggots of the mangold fly literally tunnelling their way through the leaves. The fly's lifecycle can be interrupted in two ways: by loosening the soil around affected plants and exposing the pupae for the birds to eat, or by removing and destroying leaves immediately the damage is noted.

BIG BUD MITE The tiny mites feed inside the buds of blackcurrants, causing the tissues to swell and usually preventing them from opening in spring. The mites also spread reversion, the most serious viral disease of blackcurrants, by migrating from the swollen buds around flowering time and leaving the virus behind; they then move on to infect healthy plants. The best way of controlling them, if done over several years, is to pick off all swollen buds during the winter and burn them.

BLACKFLY (see also APHID) This aphid attacks all varieties of beans, in particular the tips of broad beans (fava beans), usually forming in clusters on the plant.

BRUCHID BEETLE Resembles a weevil in appearance and is sometimes known by the incorrect name of bean beetle. The female lays her eggs on the plant and the grubs then hatch and bore into the seed, eating the inside and leaving the characteristic exit holes behind. Destroy beans found to contain grubs; applications of pyrethroids during flowering have also proved to be effective.

CABBAGE ROOT FLY The maggots feed on the roots of cabbages. Signs of their presence are a lack of growth, the plant turning a bluish colour, and a general wilting. Special collars can be purchased to put around the plant stem, which prevents the adult fly from laying its eggs down the sides of the roots. Alternatively, a chemical control can be used.

CABBAGE WHITE BUTTERFLY It is actually the caterpillars that are the problem, and they will attack all brassicas, potentially stripping them until only the skeletons of the leaves remain. Be observant and check regularly for the little clusters of yellow eggs and, when found, crush them between your fingers. Alternatively, pick off the caterpillars themselves and dispose of them. Liquid derris makes an effective spray.

CARROT ROOT FLY Most commonly attacks carrots, but also parsnips, celeriac, celery and parsley. It is not the fly itself that is the problem but its offspring. The adult is attracted by the carrot's smell and lays its eggs on the soil. The eggs then hatch and burrow down into the carrot to feed and overwinter there. Physical barriers are a good preventative, as is the companion planting of garlic or onions. Chemical controls are not a good idea.

CLEARWING MOTH Not very often seen, but the dead or dying shoots of currants and gooseberries may indicate the presence of this caterpillar. The moth lays its eggs in June and the caterpillar burrows into the shoots. Cut out infected shoots and dust with derris.

CODLING MOTH Usually affects apples. The small maggot-like caterpillars tunnel into apples leaving small brown mounds behind. A way of tackling the problem is to hang pheromone traps in trees; the scent emitted from them makes the male moth think that a female is inside. Lured into believing it will mate, it flies into the trap and is caught on the sticky paper inside. The method is claimed to have reduced the number of fertile eggs laid by 80 per cent.

CUTWORMS / LEATHERJACKETS / CHAFER GRUBS / WIREWORMS / MILLIPEDES All of these attack the roots of plants below ground. They are more commonly found in ground that was once grassed over, then brought back into cultivation. Once the soil is in regular use, they can be brought to the surface by hoeing and the birds will gladly finish them off. Only resort to inorganic controls if the problem is severe.

EARWIG Primarily scavengers, earwigs will eat just about anything, including other insects, and will attack lettuces, strawberries, celery, potatoes and seedling beans and beets, damaging sweetcorn by feeding on the silks. Resembling slug damage, but without leaving the trail of slime, they chew numerous, small, irregular holes in leaves, giving them a ragged appearance. Make simple traps from rolled-up corrugated cardboard or newspaper; cardboard tubes or short lengths of hose; canvas or boards; or even small cardboard boxes with ¼-inch holes punched in the sides near the bottom, baited with a small amount of oatmeal or bran.

EELWORM Onions, in particular, are invaded by these worms and there is no way of stopping them. Destroy all affected plants by burning them. Do not plant onions, leeks, beans, carrots or parsnips in the same soil for two years.

FLEA BEETLE A small black beetle that attacks most seedlings and soft-leaved plants. It is found mostly on turnips, swedes (rutabaga), radishes, and on most brassicas, leaving small holes in the leaves. Dust with derris.

GOOSEBERRY SAWFLY It is the caterpillar-like larvae that cause the damage and they can strip a plant in days. Attacks usually start in spring and can persist until autumn. Inspect plants regularly and pick off any larvae found. Dusting with derris may help.

LEAFHOPPERS Several leafhopper species are important agricultural pests in that they suck sap from plants. They carry viral diseases, so a systemic spray is advisable.

LEAF MINERS Several species of leaf miner may attack a wide range of vegetables in the field and in greenhouses, damaging leaves. Watch carefully for the presence of mined leaves and note problem areas. In field vegetables, sticky traps or sweep nets can be used, with biological controls in greenhouses.

MAGPIE MOTH The black-and-yellow caterpillar feeds on currants and gooseberries and can cause severe defoliation. Pick off and destroy .

MANGOLD FLY (see BEET-LEAF MINER)

MEALY CABBAGE APHID These rarely-seen insects gather on the undersides of leaves, sucking out the sap. Insecticidal soap will help to remove them.

ONION FLY It is the maggots of this fly that cause the damage, usually to onions but also to leeks, causing the plant to turn yellow and eventually die. They are normally seen just below the soil, and regular hoeing will expose the grubs giving passing birds something to eat. A treatment with derris dust when seedlings first emerge, then again two weeks later, will help to control them.

PEA / BEAN WEEVIL Being nocturnal, this pest is rarely seen, but the damage they cause on plants is very obvious, in that they eat out notches from the edges of the leaves. Dust the plant and surrounding ground with derris.

PEA MOTH   This is a common pest of peas but is only a problem between June and August. Eggs are laid when the peas come into flower and the grubs then feed inside the forming pods. A trap can be used, with a capsule that releases a species-specific sex pheromone, luring the adult males into the trap, where they stick to the sticky insert.

PEA THRIP Known also as thunder flies, thrips cause silvery patches to appear on pods, which are also distorted. Attacks are worse in dry weather.

PEAR MIDGE This tiny insect attacks the new fruitlets, turning them black, when they fall to the ground. Ensure that these are gathered up and destroyed; they contain the grubs that will hatch and re-infect the tree.

RASPBERRY BEETLE This pest attacks all briar fruit and feeds on the ripening fruit. Spray with derris when the first pink fruits appear. Blackberries need spraying as the flowers start to open, with loganberries being similarly treated after flowering.

RED SPIDER MITE This is more commonly found in greenhouses but can appear in the open during hot, dry weather. They attack cucumbers, peppers, aubergines (eggplants) and tomatoes in greenhouses and can affect French beans, courgettes (zucchini) and vegetable marrows in the open. The mites themselves are very tiny and can only just be seen with the naked eye. They weave webs on the plants and it is these that can more easily be spotted. They cause speckling and discoloration of the leaves which dry up and die. The best prevention, especially in the greenhouse, is to keep the atmosphere damp with a regular misting of water. Chemical controls are difficult and most are ineffective. A better idea is to introduce the predatory mite, *Phytoselius persimilis*, which is available from many garden centres.

SLUGS / SNAILS Will attack any soft-leaved plant. Pick off and dispose of any you find.

SWIFT MOTH The dirty white caterpillars of this moth can be very destructive. They live in the soil and feed on the roots of plants. Regular hoeing will kill some and bring others to the surface where birds will find and eat them. Destroy the affected plants by burning them.

STRAWBERRY TORTRIX MOTH
Joins several leaves together using a silken web, inside which the eggs are laid. Pick off the affected leaves and destroy. Try using an insect trap.

VINE WEEVIL
Eggs are laid near the plant stems in the summer and hatch into white, horseshoe-shaped grubs which stay in the ground only to emerge as adults the following year, typically in early June. The larvae feast on plant roots, often completely severing them from the upper stems, while the adults will also chew on the edges of leaves. Packs of microscopic worms (eelworms or nematodes) are available, which are watered into pots or open ground. The nematodes enter the grubs, poisoning them, then feed off them to increase their own numbers.

WHITEFLY
This can be a real problem, especially in the greenhouse, where it will attack any plant, and it is particularly fond of brassicas in the open. Whiteflies congregate on the undersides of leaves, depositing a sticky honeydew on which sooty mould can grow. When the leaf is touched they take off en masse, only to land on another nearby plant. For this reason they can be difficult to combat. Biological controls are effective in greenhouses, while spraying with an insecticidal soap can also produce good results. Spraying plants with jets of water will remove honeydew and sooty mould.

WOOLLY APHID
These aphids coat themselves in waxy secretions that resemble cotton wool. Infestations must be caught early, for once aphid numbers are high, and they have begun to distort and curl leaves, it is often hard to control them. This is because the curled leaves shelter them from insecticides and natural enemies.

YELLOWTAIL MOTH
The caterpillar of this moth is black with red-and-white markings. It is very hairy and can cause a skin rash if handled. It is sometimes found on raspberries, where it causes skeletonization of the foliage. It is not normally found in great numbers so it is best to pick off and destroy it.

BENEFICIAL INSECTS TO BE ENCOURAGED
Although your backyard may be an oasis of calm and serenity on the surface, appearances can be very deceiving. In fact it is a battleground where an eternal struggle between good and evil is being played out all through the growing season. Happily, there are some creatures that will come to the rescue and assist in the task of helping good to triumph!

LADYBIRD/LADYBUG
These pretty little spotted beetles, so beloved of small children, are not as innocent as they look, and their attractive appearance hides a cold killer within. They are voracious feeders, and are able to consume up to 50 aphids a day.

HOVERFLY
Hoverflies may resemble wasps, but are disguised as such to deter predators. And while the adult hoverfly is a nectar-loving pollinator, its offspring are as vicious as they are ugly. The greenish-brown, flattened little maggots are masters of camouflage, moving around undetected and bringing annihilation to unsuspecting aphid victims. Encourage hoverflies by growing marigolds and chamomile.

DRAGONFLY Sitting in a garden on a beautiful evening is a wonderful experience too often spoilt by nasty, biting insects; but there is a saviour at hand. All dragonflies are carnivorous in both the larval and adult stages of their lives, and they typically eat mosquitoes, midges and other small insects, catching their prey on the wing and dispatching them at speed. A dragonfly's ability to manoeuvre itself in many directions allows it to out-fly its prey, allowing it to hone in like an exocet missile. This beautiful and exotic creature depends on water to survive, so a garden pond will do much to attract more dragonflies to your garden.

LACEWING As the name suggests, the wings of this insect appear lace-like in appearance, with many intricate veins crossing their surface. Both the adult and the larvae of the species are always on the lookout for hapless victims. The larvae of lacewings, many of which are commonly known as antlions, appear very different from the adults, and vary greatly in shape and size depending on the species. The larvae are grub-like, with large jaws projecting from the fronts of their heads, which are used to seize their prey. The adults mainly feed on soft sap-sucking insects such as aphids and scale insects.

GROUND BEETLE Often found beneath stones, or sometimes seen scuttling along, the ground beetle is, in the main, an extremely beneficial insect, although some species could be regarded as pests. Ground beetles and their larvae are mostly carnivorous: some probably scavenge on the dead remains of insects and other invertebrates, while others feed extensively on vegetable matter, including plant seeds in particular. A few are specialized caterpillar and snail hunters, and there are others that prey on a fairly narrow range of small animals, such as aphids, springtails and mites. Most species, however, are not fussy, and a mixed diet of many different invertebrates, and often some vegetable matter, is quite normal. Ground beetles can be encouraged by providing them with a damp log pile in which to shelter.

BROWN CENTIPEDE The centipede is basically a predatory beast, and uses its speed to run down and catch a variety of other creatures, including woodlice, harvestmen, spiders, mites, springtails, beetles, and many other insects. They also eat worms and slugs. But there is something of a paradox here: the centipede is certainly doing the gardener a favour by eating slugs and leatherjackets, but how much of this is undone when it consumes garden spiders? This is a difficult conundrum, and illustrates the folly of spraying everything you see with insecticide.

CHAPTER SIX
KEEPING BEES

Although bee-keeping is a long-established commercial operation in many countries of the world, creating a source of employment for many as well as providing honey and other important by-products, it is nevertheless an activity that can be pursued by interested individuals in a small way, as little more than an interesting hobby, while at the same time producing some honey for personal use or for giving away to friends. It can also be a sociable pastime, for bee-keeping associations exist not only to provide information and advice, but also to be places where like-minded people can meet.

The idea of keeping bees is an appealing one, but will mean that far more bees than usual will inevitably soon be buzzing around. Therefore it is advisable to tell your neighbours of your intentions in advance, just in case there are any objections and so that your previous good relations with them will be maintained.

It is hardly surprising that keen gardeners should often be just as interested in bee-keeping, for it is a good way of ensuring bees visit their plants and pollinate them. To others, of course, honey is the key reason for keeping bees, and a well-managed colony, in a suitably flower-rich environment, might expect to yield about 50lbs (22.5kg) of honey a season, and possibly quite a bit more. Keeping bees for their honey is rewarding enough, but it is a rare privilege to observe one of nature's most enduring and fascinating creatures at first hand.

THE RIGHT CHOICE?

Bee-keeping won't suit everyone: although keeping bees does not require the sort of stamina or time needed to look after, say, horses or some other livestock, it nevertheless calls for certain things to be done at certain times. Emergencies or potential problems must be dealt with promptly, taking the right course of action, and the whole enterprise needs to be set up and maintained correctly to ensure a happy and successful hive. Remember, you are working with live animals that to some extent will depend on you for their welfare. Another obvious factor to

although bee-keepers tend bees and provide them with a home and even nourishment when required, these insects will never become tame or domesticated like some other 'farmed' animals. The bee-keeper needs to work with the bees, interpreting their needs and moods and reacting accordingly, while at the same time handling them with gentle firmness and confidence.

Bees live and work to a seasonal cycle, geared closely to the availability of flowers and the state of the weather. Therefore the time you spend attending to the hive will also vary. As a rule of thumb, half an hour to an hour per week needs to be spent on a colony during the summer months, but this may well reduce to fortnightly inspections as your experience grows. In winter, in temperate climates, when foraging ceases and general activity is very much reduced, most of your work is likely to be concerned with

consider is the bees themselves. The presence of a beehive or two in your garden is going to increase significantly the number of bees buzzing around the area, especially in the vicinity of the hive itself, and this may be an issue with certain family members. Then there is the fact that bees sting, and as a bee-keeper it is almost inevitable that you will get stung several times in a season, the chances of which can

be much reduced by good bee and hive management.

It would be wise to consult any neighbours whose properties are adjacent to the intended site of your hive or hives, just in case they have valid objections – such as strong allergies to bee stings. It is also advisable to check that there are no covenants, local bylaws or other restrictions preventing you from keeping bees. Remember, too, that

ABOVE LEFT: Bees turn nectar into honey, and workers must visit over 4,000 flowers to make a mere tablespoonful of honey.

OPPOSITE: Producing your own honey is immensely satisfying as well as providing an excellent food for family and friends.

maintaining your bee-keeping equipment. But remember that there is honey to harvest and process, not to mention gathering and using some of the beeswax, all of which take time. But then, wasn't this all part of the attraction in the first place?

MAKING A START

Before going to the trouble and expense of getting the bees for your hive and buying all the necessary equipment – and indeed, there is plenty of it on offer to tempt the unwary – it is worth attending demonstrations, such as those often held by local bee-keeping associations. Here you will see exactly what is involved in opening the hive and handling the bees, and there will, of course, be opportunities to ask knowledgeable and experienced bee-keepers to answer the questions that have been bothering you.

It may even be possible to handle bees yourself so that you can experience exactly what to expect at first hand. This may well be the moment when you discover that the prospect of potentially venomous little creatures, wandering all over your body (even if you are wearing protective clothing), is not to your liking, and that bee-keeping is not for

you after all. But if you relish the thought and decide to proceed, make a note of the people present who may best advise you later on. It will also be of benefit to join one of the bee-keeping organizations in your area, or enrol in a starter course in bee-keeping, perhaps through a local bee-keeping club, which is a valuable way to approach the subject in the correct manner.

It is necessary to consider the best place in which to position a hive before you purchase any equipment, and then set about preparing the site in anticipation of its arrival. It goes without saying that the hive should be placed on firm, dry, weed-free ground. A well-ventilated sunny aspect is also ideal, perhaps one that faces south or east. Locate the hive away from danger of frost, dripping water and wind, if possible. Don't forget that you will need comfortable access to the hive yourself, and a hive stand will make the task that much easier; some hives come with legs

LEFT & OPPOSITE: Before embarking on your own bee-keeping venture, it is important to seek the best expert advice available and even to attend lessons, when the instructor will demonstrate the correct way to handle bees and also advise on the best equipment to buy.

OPPOSITE: Children are certain to be fascinated by bees, but must be closely supervised at all times.

ABOVE: Bees can be kept successfully in all kinds of different locations, and will also prove to be of immense benefit to the environment in general.

already attached and these may give you all the height you need. The stand must be tall enough to keep the hive out of reach of marauding animals and strong enough to support the weight of a healthy colony, which may eventually reach about 150lbs (70kg) or so. You can also make a hive stand out of

breeze blocks, bricks or stout timber, which should be about 2–3ft (0.6–0.9m) high. This allows you to access the hive without having to bend too much and will keep the hive itself clear of damp ground. Whatever system you use, make sure that the hive is secure on its stand and cannot wobble or, worse still, blow over in a strong wind. Don't forget that you may need to access the hive from all sides, so position it with plenty of space surrounding it. You will also need to ensure that the hive entrance doesn't become obscured by weeds and other plant growth.

Fresh water must be available at all times; if there is no natural source of water close by, then one must be provided. This can be a moderately large, shallow dish sited off the ground, a shallow-sided bird bath being ideal for the purpose; but whatever is used must allow the bees access to the water without the danger of them falling in and drowning. If possible, screen your hive to prevent it from becoming an eyesore for neighbours, and remember that the bees' flightpath should be as far as possible from places where you or your neighbours are likely to congregate; no one wants squadrons of foraging bees flying across their patios while they are enjoying their garden.

RIGHT: The head must be thoroughly protected at all times.

OPPOSITE: The correct clothing does much to make bee-keeping a pleasurable occupation while also keeping safe.

The flightpath should also avoid roads, and a tall fence or some natural plant cover, such as evergreens planted close to the hive, will ensure the bees' flight takes them high and away from hazards when approaching and leaving the hive, thus minimizing disturbance. And finally, it goes without saying that if it wasn't already, your garden should now become an insecticide-free zone, for insecticide-laden sprays can also be blown towards hives by the wind as well as covering adjacent plants.

BASIC EQUIPMENT
There is equipment galore available from a myriad of suppliers, although much of it will prove unnecessary for the beginner or even for the experienced small-scale bee-keeper. But once you have decided exactly what you do need, be sure to buy the best

ABOVE & OPPOSITE: It is sometimes useful to work with another person, but remember that even interested bystanders should also be well-protected.

you can afford and then look after it so that it will give you many years of reliable service. It is certainly worth checking the prices of similar items before finally deciding to buy. Make sure you order or obtain all the equipment that is really necessary beforehand, so that everything is to hand once the hive is set up and running. For instance, it's no good wondering how to feed a nucleus of hungry bees after they have been delivered. For this reason, let's start with the essential equipment before considering the hive itself.

PROTECTIVE CLOTHING

To reduce the chances of being stung and to keep your clothes clean while tending to the hive, either a beesuit or a bee tunic or jacket, available from bee-keeping suppliers, is an essential item. A beesuit is a one-piece unit intended to cover and protect the entire body and which resembles one of the spacesuits worn by astronauts. The drawbacks of beesuits are that they are cumbersome and can be uncomfortable to wear in hot weather. A bee tunic or jacket protects the head, upper body and arms, and should have elasticated sleeves. With this form of clothing, you

will, of course, need to make provision for protecting your legs by wearing some loose-fitting strong trousers, that can be tucked snugly into your boots; in this respect, a pair of rubber 'Wellington'-type boots are ideal, but make sure they are wide enough at the tops to take your trousers and provide a gap-free fit when they are tucked

inside. Whatever style of clothing you have, it is best to choose a hood and veil (to protect your head and face) that can be detached by a zipper or similar secure method to prevent bees from getting inside. You can, of course, improvise by choosing a wide-brimmed hat with a fine mesh securely sewn to the brim all the way round. The mesh

must be sufficiently long to be tucked in securely at the neck so that bees cannot enter at this point. Most proprietary protective clothing tends to be white, with a darker-coloured mesh or veil for protecting the face. There is a reason for this: in the wild, the bees' natural hive-raiding enemies include bears, skunks and other predators. These tend to be brown or black in colour, so white or light-coloured clothing helps the bees to distinguish the bee-keeper from their usual enemies.

Gloves are an essential item for the beginner, even though they can restrict movement and tend eventually to be discarded by more experienced keepers. Appropriate gloves are available from suppliers, but a pair of strong, close-fitting rubber gloves are a good substitute. Some stores sell strong but supple gloves for general maintenance and DIY, which may also be suitable, but the purpose-made gauntlets, that go some way up the wearer's sleeves, offer the greater protection.

OPPOSITE & RIGHT: The smoker is an essential piece of equipment; it produces smoke that calms the bees, making inspection of the hive that much easier.

SMOKERS

An essential item of equipment as far as the bee-keeper is concerned. There is quite a variation in quality and ease of use in respect of smokers, so try to look at and compare a few different types before making a final choice. A smoker is a device used to puff smoke into the colony with the purpose of calming the bees so that the hive can be inspected more easily. It is shaped rather like a coffee pot, and it is essentially a metal can with a spout at the top and a grate at the bottom in which fuel is burned (to make the smoke); there is a simple bellows arrangement attached to it so that the smoke can be forced out of the spout. Choose a larger rather that smaller one, and be sure it has a guard around it to prevent the hot sides of the device from touching you or your clothing. Some smokers have quite stiff bellows, making them difficult to

LEFT: The calming effects of smoke on bees has been known for centuries, and when used properly is an effective way to approach them safely.

OPPOSITE: The hive tool has a number of uses and is a vital piece of equipment. It can be used as a lever, scraper or hook.

operate, so opt for one with a nice smooth action.

A variety of fuels can be burned in the smoker: ready-prepared fuels can be bought from bee-keeping equipment suppliers or you can use your own, or a mixture of both. Commercially available fuels include rolls of corrugated cardboard, cotton waste, hessian, old sacking and compressed pellets of wood chips. Your own fuels might consist of sawdust, dried and crumbled natural timber (for example, rotten wood), pine needles and so on. Old building timber, cut up and pulped, can also be used, but never use anything on which an insecticide or wood preservative has been used, since the fumes from such items can be toxic to both bees and human beings.

For this reason, avoid using pieces of wood from decking and fence offcuts, since many of these have been commercially pre-treated using harmful chemicals. Whatever fuels you choose, always use them in accordance with the instructions supplied with the smoker, and check first with an experienced bee-keeper or someone from one of the bee associations if there is any doubt. It goes without saying that young children should be allowed nowhere near a working smoker.

So how does the smoke work? The calming effect of smoke on bees has been known since ancient times. First, smoke masks the pheromones that are the bees' chief means of mass communication and which are used by guard or injured bees to alert the hive to potential danger, such as when it is being opened. This breakdown of communication, and thus the chain of command and action, gives the bee-keeper an opportunity to check the hive and close it again without too much disruption to the occupants. The smoke also seems to initiate a feeding response in the bees, presumably because it triggers them to prepare for abandonment of the hive; therefore, they are stoking up on food to be used when the colony first re-establishes itself somewhere safer. Also, a fully engorged bee is less likely to sting, so smoke has another positive effect in protecting the bee-keeper. Using the smoker correctly is an acquired art, and the inexperienced bee-keeper should not be surprised or dismayed if the technique fails to work as it should at first. Small, well-directed puffs of smoke, rather than a massive smokescreen, are what you are trying to achieve.

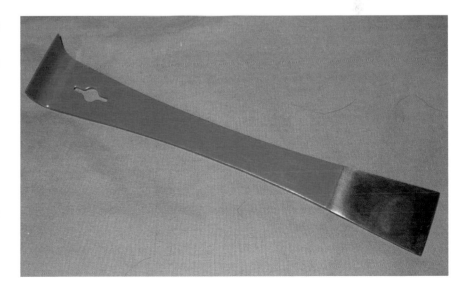

LEFT: The hive tool should always be to hand.

OPPOSITE: These beehives have been sited in a field of lavender, both to promote pollination and to produce a unique honey with a wonderful flavour and aroma.

HIVE TOOLS

The hive tool is a specially designed piece of equipment that is used as lever, scraper and hook. The tool comes made from wood or stainless steel, and is often brightly coloured since it seems to end up frequently getting lost. It is used when dismantling the hive and when removing frames from it, the scraper part being utilized to remove build-ups of propolis from parts of the hive. Such a range of functions would suggest a complex tool, but in fact the design is quite simple. One of the best types (about 10in /25cm long) resembles an elongated version of the kind of scraper used to remove ice from car windows in winter. One end is flat, broad and sharpened and acts as a scraper, and the other is curved, with a slot near the end, and is used as a lever. When using the tool to separate parts of the hive, the curved end of the tool is placed between adjacent frame-top bars and twisted to left or right.

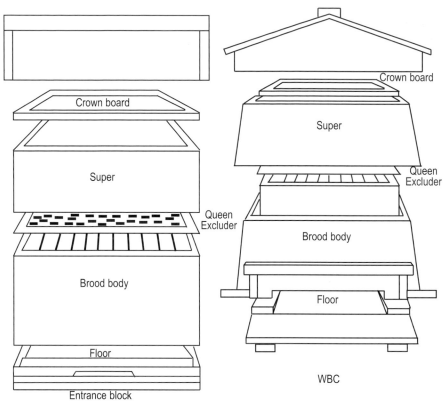

Crown board

Super

Queen Excluder

Floor

Entrance block

LANGSTROTH

Crown board

Super

Queen Excluder

Brood body

Floor

Entrance block

NATIONAL

Crown board

Super

Queen Excluder

Brood body

Floor

WBC

Levering is achieved by lipping the curved part under the item to be lifted and then pressing down on the other end. The hole in the tool is intended for

removing nails, but is also a convenient place to attach a cord so that the tool can be tied to your belt, making it conveniently to hand when required.

Hives

The hive is clearly an extremely important item of a bee-keeper's equipment, for it is the place where the

honeybees will live and from which honey and other bee products will be harvested. Like so much else in life, beginners can easily be confused by the available choice and may ultimately be seduced by an attractive design, a keen price, or even a supplier's sales patter, and thus buy the wrong type of hive for their purpose. You will soon see that several different types are available, both new and secondhand, some of

160

OPPOSITE ABOVE: Cross-sections of Langstroth, National and WBC beehives.

OPPOSITE LEFT: The frames on which the bees will make their honeycomb.

ABOVE: A bee-keeper working on his Langstroth hives.

which are offered ready-assembled, with others coming 'flat-packed' for home assembly. The 'Langstroth' is used almost exclusively in the United States, but also appears in Britain and other parts of the world, while popular hives in Britain are marketed under names such as 'WBC', 'Commercial' and 'National'. The most popular hives are made of wood, though artificial materials, such as polystyrene, are also used. Cedarwood is a popular choice in temperate climates, since it is very durable yet light in weight. Secondhand hives carry the risk of being infected with foulbrood, a disease of honeybees

caused by the bacterium *Melissococcus plutonius* or by the more virulent *Paenibacillus larvae*. If there is any doubt concerning the provenance of such a hive then it is advisable to steer clear of it altogether.

Hives are constructed as a series of boxes, each carrying suspended frames on which the bees build their combs.

Above these brood-frame boxes there can normally be fitted a meshlike device known as a queen excluder, the mesh allowing the workers to pass through freely while restricting the queen because of her larger size. Because she cannot access any frames above the queen excluder, she cannot lay eggs in them, and they are therefore used only for storing the honey. Frames or boxes used for storing honey are called 'supers', and they are obviously of great interest to the honey-collecting

OPPOSITE: National beehives.

ABOVE: Attractive WBC hives sited at the bottom of a country garden.

bee-keeper. By altering the position of the queen excluder, a bee-keeper can decide how many boxes to allocate to the brood section or to the super section of the hive. (In the active part of the season, when there are plenty of flowers from which to forage, many bee-keepers consider it worth having two supers in use at the same time.)

Each frame consists of a four-sided structure somewhat like a picture frame. Frames may be made of wood or plastic, within which there is either a beeswax-covered plastic foundation sheet, embossed with a honeycomb pattern, or a sheet of honeycomb-

OPPOSITE LEFT: Hives sited in an apple orchard to ensure pollination and the production of fruit.

OPPOSITE RIGHT: A colourfully painted WBC hive.

RIGHT: Before the onset of winter, hives may be placed in a more sheltered position to protect them from cold winds. In very cold climates, the beehives may be brought into a barn or shed in winter.

embossed pure beeswax set on a wire frame. In either case, the bees build their comb on the foundation sheet. It is advisable not to mix frames in the same box that have been used by bees for brood-rearing and food storage.

At the top of the uppermost box there should be an inner cover. This allows for a gap between the outer top covering of the hive and the hive itself, and helps the airflow as well as preventing heat from the outer cover acting directly on the hive in hot weather. Also, without the inner cover, there is a tendency for the bees to seal the outer cover to the top frame with propolis, making its removal difficult. Even the inner cover will need to be removed with the flat blade of a hive

tool, but this is an easier prospect than levering under the outer cover. To avoid the need to ease the inner cover off, some bee-keepers lay a sheet of canvas over the top frame instead, which can be rolled back when it is necessary to inspect the bees.

Another device is a clearer or an escape board. This is designed to remove the bees from the supers down to the lower boxes and prevent them from returning. This allows the supers to be removed for honey extraction.

The outer cover is a durable waterproof structure at the top of the hive boxes that keeps the weather out. It is usually constructed from wood or plastic. At the base of the hive there is a bottom board with a place for the bees to enter and leave, and usually a platform or ramp that acts as a landing stage and waiting area so that incoming bees can be inspected by the guards. Some bottom boards are fitted with screens to allow debris to fall clear of the hive and to increase the ventilation within.

LEFT: Bees coming and going as they please.

OPPOSITE: An exposed hive showing the individual frames.

A competent **DIY** enthusiast can easily make a serviceable hive themselves, but it is recommended that good-quality plans and dimensions are followed rather than merely copying a diagram from a book; although the overall size of the hive is somewhat unimportant, some of the internal dimensions, spacings and structural details are critical if the hive is to be fully effective. For example, there must be the correct space at the tops of the frames so that the bees can walk about, but not so much that they start building combs there. Take heed of advice concerning the treatment of the surfaces, so that nothing toxic is used that could harm the bees.

Suppliers also sell specially designed and safe weather coatings for use on hive exteriors.

Many authorities recommend beginners start with a hive consisting of three or four medium-depth frames, but once some experience has been gained, and there is an expanding colony, more can be added.

FEEDERS

Feeders are devices that dispense food to bees in the form of sugar syrup. They come in a variety of forms: hive-top feeders are designed to replace the inner cover on the top of the hive, and are made of wood or plastic. They hold up to about 2 gallons (9 litres) of sugar syrup, and can be used at the end of the year to feed the colony. The design of the feeder prevents bees from getting into the sugar solution and drowning. Hive-top feeders can be left in position all year. A small bucketlike feeder is also available, which fit over the hole that is a feature of some inner covers, then a couple of supers are placed over to cover it. Another type, called a

ABOVE: Checking the comb for bee larvae.

OPPOSITE: Still-life with smoker.

Boardman or an entrance feeder, has an arrangement that enables an inverted jar of the syrup to be placed near the hive entrance, so that the bees can feed on it there. Although this

system allows bees from other colonies to steal the syrup, it enables you to see how much food is being taken and to top it up without opening up the hive every time. Then there is a frame feeder, which replaces one of the normal types of frames suspended in the boxes.

OTHER EQUIPMENT

A few other items of equipment will be of help in your bee-keeping endeavours. First of these is a record book, because good record-keeping is important and may be of future value. For a start, it may remind you when you need to do certain tasks, or watch out for particular aspects of bee behaviour. The things that didn't go to plan can also be noted, also the need for them to be revised. It is also useful to have details of the suppliers of your queen and other bees to hand, as well as those of other suppliers, organizations, people you can contact in the event of an emergency or from whom to seek general advice. The date each visit to the hive is made should also be recorded, together with weather conditions, temperature, and so on current at the time. At the same time, behaviour in the hive and the general temperament of the colony should also be noted down (for example, are the bees quiet or agitated?), while it may be useful to record the number of queen cells, the number of drones present and the general condition of the combs and of the hive itself. When making a visit, note down what tasks you undertook, including the amount of honey harvested.

Special equipment is required for collecting and storing honey (see pages 185 et seq.), but with regard to harvesting it, again it is valuable to keep a note of when this was done, the amount of honey collected, and any other relevant details, such as the price at which it was sold.

As you progress, you will probably find that a few items, such as a hammer, some pliers and a ball of string, will come in useful. It's worth

LEFT: Bee feeders resemble water dispensers.

OPPOSITE: It is time to source your bees once all your equipment is assembled in place.

keeping these together in a small tool bag or roll so that they are with you when tending the hive. Any other items proving their worth can be included as you go along.

OBTAINING BEES

In the same way that bee-keeping equipment can be obtained from specialist suppliers, so it will be when you acquire your actual bees. Rather like bee-keeping equipment, there are good bees and bad bees, so it pays to choose carefully. 'Bad' bees may be difficult temperamentally, making handling them a more irksome task than it should be, or they may come with brood diseases or may simply be inefficient gatherers, with the result that honey yields may suffer. Your first port of call might usefully be your local bee-keeping association, which will put you in touch with a bee-keeper in your area who has some good, surplus bees available; but first get some assurances regarding the quality of the stock and, if possible, some recommendations concerning the bee-keeper in question. The advantages of obtaining a colony in this way is that it will already be established and ready to go, and will be acclimatized to the local area. By the

same token, however, it means that there is no 'starting-up period' whereby confidence can be gained as the colony grows – it's all action from the word go. Make sure these same bees come from hives which are at least 3 miles (4.8km)

from the place where you intend to site your own hive, otherwise the bees may simply return to their original home when released from your hive.

The most popular course of action, however, is to obtain stock either from the supplier from which all or some of your equipment came, or from a recognized professional breeder of bees. The bees acquired from one of these sources are much more likely to be good stock, and a reputable breeder shouldn't object to having his bees inspected for disease by an expert before purchase.

Of the different ways to buy bees, first, it is possible to buy a complete colony. This consists of ten or so combs and contains a fertile queen, workers and, depending on the time of year, drones. The whole thing should come complete with stores of food and a brood (developing bees, including eggs, larvae and pupae). Obtaining such a colony in, say, May or June, should make it possible for the colony to produce surplus honey in the first year.

The second method is to buy what is known as a nucleus, which is a small colony consisting of between four and six combs containing a fertile queen,

some workers and perhaps some drones. It also includes some food and brood. A nucleus is a much smaller proposition than the complete colony described previously, and will be easier for the beginner to handle. Once installed within the hive the nucleus will, of course, develop into a complete colony, and may even produce a little honey in the first year.

A third route is to obtain what is called a package. This is a screened or meshed box simply containing honeybees and a queen. Once delivered from the breeder, you must transfer the bees into your own hive and feed them so that they get off to a quick start. The other option is to obtain a natural swarm of bees, which is a free-living colony without any combs. Early swarms tend to develop well since they have the whole flowering season ahead of them, but late swarms will require plenty of feeding or they will fail to survive the winter. The other issue regarding swarms is that, unless its origin, good health and good temper can be proven, it may turn out to be a bad group of bees.

OPPOSITE: Never attempt to catch a natural swarm of bees yourself: leave it to the experts.

ABOVE RIGHT: Bees may be purchased in what is called a package, and which contains honeybees and a queen.

RIGHT: Bees should by bought from a reputable supplier to ensure they are healthy and temperamentally sound.

Assuming that the decision to keep bees has now been made, you will have read all that can reasonably be expected about the subject; you will have attended some bee-keeping sessions; and you have had all the necessary discussions with family and neighbours. You have probably even chosen the site and have invested in the necessary equipment, such as the hive, the tools, protective clothing and so on. Now, also assuming that it is spring or early

ABOVE: Healthy bees are more likely to produce plenty of honey. These bees are on a Langstroth frame.

OPPOSITE: The ultimate aim: delicious golden honey.

summer, it is time to acquire your first batch of bees by one of the methods already described.

TRANSFERRING BEES INTO THE HIVE

Let's assume, first of all, that you have bought a nucleus. The supplier may give instructions on how to transfer the nucleus and the frames to your hive and how to provide any other immediate requirements, such as food for the bees. Before taking delivery of the nucleus, check with the supplier so that you know what to do when it arrives.

The essential procedures are as follows: when the nucleus arrives, place it on the hive stand, open the entrance and allow the bees to fly about for an hour or two. Next, take the nucleus off the hive stand and replace it with the hive. Remove the lid of the nucleus and give a puff or two of smoke from the smoker. Using your frame tool, prise apart the frames (you may need another puff or two of smoke to keep the bees out of the way as you do this). Lift each frame from the nucleus in turn and place it in the lowermost brood box, keeping the frames in the same sequence. Fill any empty frame spaces with new foundation frames. Put the inner cover on. A feeder

with about 1 1/2 –3 pints (1–2 litres) of sugar syrup should be placed over the feed hole before adding the outer cover. The queen excluder and the first honey super can be installed about a month later, assuming the colony is becoming established in full season.

Alternatively, you may have decided to purchase a package of bees. A typical package weighs about 3lbs (1.4kg) and

consists of approximately 3,500 bees. The queen will probably be in a separate queen cage within the package, and the worker bees will be clustered around the cage. Expect to see a few dead bees on the floor of the package box, but if the numbers seem excessive, contact the supplier. If the bees have exhausted their food supply, lightly spray a sugar solution (one-third sugar to two-thirds water in warm water) into the box using a mister. The bees must merely be moistened rather than saturated; don't leave them in the box for any longer than is necessary once they have been delivered, but transfer them to the hive as soon as it is practicable and providing the weather is not too cold. Late afternoon or early evening is a good time to do this.

Before putting the bees into the hive, make sure you have all your equipment to hand, that you are wearing your protective clothing, and that the smoker is lit. You may also need a pair

of pliers. Remove the feeder from the package box, then remove the queen cage from the box. Remove any fixings from the feeder, then lift the box and bang it on the ground so that any bees attached to the feeder fall off. Next, remove the queen cage and shake or blow off any bees attached to it. Make sure the queen is alive and looking healthy. At this stage, the queen cage can be inserted into the hive by pushing it between the frames in the centre of the lowermost hive box. Ensure that the mesh side faces downwards and that the workers can make contact with the queen. Within the queen cage is a section containing a sugar mixture that must usually be pierced with a pin or small nail.

Now place a second hive box on top of the first one, then remove some of the frames to make a space in which to dump the bees. Get the bees out of the package box by banging the box again, removing the cover and shaking or

OPPOSITE: These bees are well-established in their hives and are coming and going at will.

ABOVE RIGHT: It is possible to buy an established bee colony which can be transported to your own hive.

'pouring' the bees downwards into the hive. Use the smoker to gently coax them down if necessary. You won't get every single bee out by this method, but when most of them are out, put the package box by the side of the hive so that the rest can come out in their own time, then carefully replace the missing frames from the hive box, trying not to trap any bees as you do so. Now replace the rest of the hive boxes and their frames and the inner and outer covers, attaching a sugar syrup feeder to the hive.

INSPECTING THE HIVE

Assuming sufficient food has been supplied when first inserting the bees, allow the colony to settle down for three days before inspecting the hive. On opening up the hive, first check the activity of the bees surrounding the queen (don't use smoke before opening the hive because you want to observe the bees' natural reactions). If they seem generally calm, with only a few bees on the cage, it is probably safe now to release the queen. But if her cage is still completely surrounded by bees that are reluctant to be removed, close the hive up and wait for two more days.

When it seems safe to remove the queen, take off the plug covering the queen cage sugar mixture and make sure that the hole is clear by poking it with a pin or small nail. Replace the queen cage between the frames. In a few days, the workers will have eaten enough of the sugar mixture for the queen to be released. (Some bee-keepers simply release the queen directly from her cage into the hive during the first inspection, but only if all seems well.) Refill the feeder and close up the hive. A couple of days

BELOW: After a few days, and when the bees have calmed down, the queen can be released.

OPPOSITE: Discovering eggs is a good sign that the colony is becoming established.

later, check that the workers have released the queen. If not, release her yourself by opening up her cage and letting her join the other hive members.

GETTING GOING

The queen should begin laying about a week after her release. The eggs are tiny white structures resembling miniature grains of sand, and they should be visible within some of the cells built by the worker bees. Discovering eggs is a good sign that all is well and that the colony is beginning to take off and get established. At this stage, keep the feeder topped up, but otherwise leave things alone for about ten days. If, however, no eggs are visible, despite your searches, first make sure that the queen is still present. If she is, it is possible that she wasn't mated before you got her, or that she is in some way unable to lay eggs. When this happens, the only course of action is to replace her with another queen.

As the colony develops and egg-laying proceeds, and as the workers continue to build their comb on the frames of the available boxes, you will need to add a new box of frames as the existing ones get built upon. It may also be necessary to swap around some of

the frames in the existing boxes so that they all get used. At this stage, keep using the feeder to supplement the bees' food supply. Make sure you always have sufficient supers ready for when the production of honey begins in earnest. The best advice is always to be aware of what is happening inside the hive with regard to brood, comb-production and honey storage, adjusting the number of frames you provide accordingly. External conditions should also be taken into account: for example, what is the

weather like? Is it conducive to bee activity? Are there plenty of local blooms available?

INSPECTING THE ESTABLISHED COLONY

There is often much to do when the hive is opened and, especially for the novice confronted by bees upset by the invasion of their home, it can be difficult to remember why you are inspecting the hive in the first place. Try to memorize the following before opening up:

• Does everything seem normal? Are the bees fairly active? Is there evidence of disease present? (Admittedly, such questions may only be answered adequately with experience.)

• Does the colony have enough food?

• Is all the space being filled? Is another super needed?
• Is the queen laying eggs? Is there older brood as well as eggs?

• Can you see new queen cells? Is the colony going to swarm?

The first task is to get the smoker lit and burning well. Have any equipment you may need to hand, such as the hive tool, together with the feeders and extra supers or brood frames you may wish to add. Don your protective clothing. Begin by introducing a small puff of smoke through the entrance door of the hive, then wait for a minute or so. Now you must remove the outer cover from the top of the hive. Lift an edge of the inner cover first; sometimes this will need a bit of encouragement, so use the end of your hive tool, puffing a little smoke into the gap you have made. Carefully lift off the cover completely.

Now you will see the inside of the topmost box. If the colony is still new, there may be little or no comb-building activity, but there will probably be some bees around. Lift a corner of the box and puff in some smoke. Now lift the box off completely and lay it carefully on the ground. Puff some smoke onto the top to prevent the bees from flying off. If the colony is going well, the next box you examine will probably show more signs of activity, particularly comb build-up in the centremost frames.

To examine a frame in detail, carefully lift it out of the box. It is best to begin by examining frames near to the outer edges of the box. Puff a small amount of smoke over the top of the box. Loosen the frame, if necessary, by gently levering or twisting the hive tool between two frames. Lift the frame out of the box, keeping it straight and taking care not to injure, trap or inadvertently kill any bees. If there is no comb build-up on the frame, place it by the hive entrance for the time being

OPPOSITE: Have your hive tool to hand when inspecting the hive...

RIGHT: ... also your smoker.

the tropics, where warmer temperatures prevail. Below is a general account of the hive year.

In late winter, as the days begin to lengthen, the queen begins or increases her egg-laying activity. The workers consume the hive's stored supply of pollen and honey to produce food for the developing brood. In early spring the first flowers become available to help supplement the hive's store of food, and the brood is beginning to increase rapidly. The expanding hive population may well trigger the start of swarming behaviour at this time. In temperate regions, swarms usually occur from April to June.

By early summer, nectar and pollen are readily available in temperate regions, although they may start to decline in the tropics. Late summer sees another burst of nectar- and pollen-collecting activity in temperate regions. This is the period of major honey production.

to allow the bees to return to the hive. Follow the same procedure and lift out the next frame. If this frame shows signs of comb-building, check to see if there are any eggs. Hold the frame and its comb up over the hive (in case the queen is there and falls off) so that sunlight can shine on the cells, making the task easier. Then carefully replace the frame, taking care not to crush bees as you put it back and ensuring that it is positioned correctly. When replacing a box, it is better to slide it into position rather than drop it onto a lower box. By doing this, you are encouraging the bees to move out of

the way, avoiding crushing them. When you are ready, replace the inner cover, the feeder (if being used) and the outer cover. The whole process of examination should take no longer than 15 minutes or so once you have become proficient at the task.

THE HIVE YEAR

The bees involve themselves in different activities according to the seasons, although these will naturally vary according to the hive's geographical location. For example, bee behaviour in temperate parts of the world won't be quite the same as that of bees living in

ABOVE LEFT: In winter, the bees cluster together in the hive to keep warm.

OPPOSITE: In spring, the first flowers appear, ready to supplement the hive's dwindling store of food.

When November arrives, most plant-flowering is over for the year and the colony starts to slow down. By winter the colony begins to cluster together to keep warm, the bees beating their wings to generate additional heat and feeding off their stored food reserves. On warmer winter days the bees may break their cluster to access the food in other parts of the hive, or even go out on cleansing flights.

THE BEE-KEEPING YEAR

Whatever the time of year, there is always something for the bee-keeper to do. Here is a month-by-month summary of bee-keeping duties, although the timing of various tasks and events will, to an extent, be governed by local conditions. The record book should be kept up to date at all times.

DECEMBER–FEBRUARY
• Check for hive damage caused by woodpeckers, squirrels or other animals, and repair as needed.

KEEPING BEES

- Check roof isn't leaking.
- Ensure hive entrance isn't blocked with debris or dead bees.
- Make sure the hive still slopes slightly forward to avoid rainwater accumulating on the top. Wedge the bottom of the hive at the back to ensure correct angle.
- Feed bees as necessary.
- Check condition of screening, hive tool, etc.
- Attend bee-keeping courses, meetings, and so on.

MARCH
- Increase feeding.
- Continue to check for hive damage and repair as needed.

APRIL
- Continue feeding with sugar syrup.
- Replace the floor with a clean one.
- Add a new super, if required, and fit the queen excluder.
- Apply varroa mite treatment.
- Be aware of any early swarming activity.

BELOW and OPPOSITE: Honey is stored in the honeycomb cells.

MAY
- Regular inspections of the brood comb should start now. Replace old brood comb (about one-third of the brood comb will probably require replacement throughout the season).
- Check there is sufficient food in the brood chamber.
- Add any supers that may be required.
- Remove varroa treatment before honey begins to flow.

JUNE
- Check brood frames and replace any that are damaged.
- Continue to check for signs of swarming.
- Remove any frames that have wax-capped honey, and replace with new ones and/or additional supers.

JULY–AUGUST
- End of swarming.
- Remove queen excluder in August.
- Start to harvest honey in August.
- Reduce entrance with entrance block to prevent wasps from entering.
- Insert varroa strips for 42 days.

SEPTEMBER
• Begin feeding colony, using sugar solution with a nosema disease-killing agent such as Fumidil B.
• Remove varroa strips.
• Fit a mouse guard to the hive entrance.

OCTOBER–DECEMBER
• Ensure the hive is secure and cannot blow over in winter winds.
• Ensure entrance is cleared of dead bees (the mouse guard will restrict the entrance somewhat).

HONEY AND OTHER BEE PRODUCTS

Bees may be kept simply for the pleasure of caring for them, becoming involved in their world, and to help to increase declining honeybee populations. But chances are that the main reason is to have a ready supply of honey – and perhaps beeswax. In the same way that there are well-established rules for tending bees, it is important to follow the correct procedures when harvesting honey. Remember that a foodstuff is being handled and prepared, some or all of which may be sold on to the public. You must therefore ensure that everything is kept

scrupulously clean and that regulations applying to the sale of honey in your area are strictly adhered to.

HARVESTING HONEY

Numerous books and websites are devoted to the subject of harvesting, extracting and putting honey into jars, but below is a general account of the process, which describes the main stages and the options available. Honey extraction is a somewhat messy business requiring a few pieces of specialized equipment, some method of temperature regulation, and a little know-how. Should you decide this aspect of bee-keeping is not for you, other bee-keepers may be willing to perform the task for you.

You will know when it is time to begin collecting the honey because the supers will have their honeycombs closed off with wax coverings. Get your smoker lit, put on your protective clothing and have your hive tool to hand. The first job is to get all the bees out of the super, or supers, from which the honey is to be obtained. To facilitate this, a bee escape is used. This is a board that is placed under the super you wish to remove. It contains an exit that allows the bees to move down into the brood area, but prevents them from returning to the honey super. Give the bees 24 hours to vacate the super. Some bee-keepers use a fume board to encourage them to leave; this is a special board with a cloth impregnated with a safe chemical, such as benzaldehyde or butric anhydride, the first of which smells like bitter almonds, and which can be obtained from bee-keeping suppliers. When a fume board is used, it normally takes

BELOW: The honey is ready for harvesting when the honeycomb has been capped off with wax.

OPPOSITE LEFT: A disassembled bee escape.

OPPOSITE RIGHT: The bees can be encouraged to leave the super by using a blower. The novice is advised to wear gloves.

only a quarter of an hour or so for the bees to leave; the chemical is not

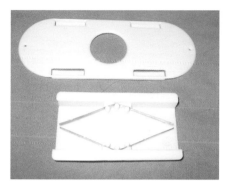

poisonous to them, they merely find it offensive. Another method is to use a mechanical blower to forcibly remove the bees from the super, having first removed it from the hive. The super should be placed on top of the hive with the bottom of it facing the back of the hive before a blast is directed through the frames. In any case, a light smoking is useful to begin the evacuation process.

EXTRACTING AND BOTTLING HONEY

Once the bees have vacated the box, the frames containing the honey can be removed. Honey extraction should be carried out in a clean room using clean materials; the honey will flow better if the temperature is warm. In many ways a kitchen is the ideal place, being warm and with access to power and running

water. This may not accord with everyone's idea of what a kitchen should be used for, however, and so a utility room or even a garage may have to double up as an extraction room, provided it is not adjacent to a lavatory. Hands must be thoroughly clean, with waterproof dressings covering cuts, and clean protective clothing must be worn. Clean up as you go along.

All equipment must be of food-grade plastic or stainless steel. First get a bucket and place some cheese cloth inside it, allowing some of the material to drape over the edges. Now place a piece of wood approximately 3 x 2in (7.5 x 5cm) thick across the top of the bucket. A couple of notches cut out to make it fit the rim of the bucket without slipping around, and another on the opposite side to hold the frame securely, will greatly assist the task that follows. Now, resting one end of the frame on the piece of wood, cut or carve off the wax cappings that seal the comb, leaning the frame slightly at an angle so that the cappings fall off without sticking back onto the frame lower down. A proprietory uncapping knife (some are heated to make the task easier) or a sharp, strong carving knife are suitable for the purpose, using the

two edges of the frame as cutting guides. You will see the capping fall into the bucket. The honey that flows out with the cappings can be gathered once it has drained through the cloth. Once you have completed one side, turn the frame over and do the same with the other side. Once the process is understood, more efficient ways of collecting and straining the honey may be devised – perhaps a plastic box with a fine filter can be used, set above a second box with a tap built into the side near the bottom to allow the collected honey to flow out.

The honeycomb should now be placed in an extractor, of which there are several types, chief among them being the radial and the tangential, named according to the way the frames are held in the unit. Both, however, extract the honey by using centrifugal force – rather like the action of a spin-drier removing water. The best extractors are made from food-grade polythene or stainless steel; other

OPPOSITE: Remove the wax cappings from the frame using a specialist knife or a carving knife.

RIGHT: The honey extractor uses centrifugal force to remove the honey from the comb.

materials are not suitable for honey that is intended for public consumption. Some extractors are driven by electric motors and others are operated by turning a handle. It is also possible to hire a good extractor from bee-keeping associations rather than

ABOVE & RIGHT: The honey is drained from the extractor via a strainer.

OPPOSITE: The honey can be poured into sterilized jars once it has been strained.

buying one. Always follow the manufacturer's instructions, paying attention to the way the extractor is loaded and cleaned after use.

The honey should then be finely strained directly from the extractor, a task made easier if it is warm, bearing in mind that once the honey starts to granulate it will not pass through a sieve unless it is warmed. The strained honey is collected in a bucket prior to bottling. The best way to remove honey from the bucket is by means of a tap, called a honey gate, and it is an easy task to fit one yourself, nylon honey gates, with the necessary washers and fixings, being readily available. Cut a hole near to the bottom of a plastic bucket and fit on the honey gate. Again, you will need to warm the honey so that it flows easily out of the bucket and into jars. If you are competent at DIY, a simple way to do this is to build a warming box comprising a couple of electric light bulbs (each about 40W). Place the buckets on the warming box until the honey is of the desired consistency but without overheating it.

Jars must be perfectly clean and dry and preferably sterilized by filling each clean jar with water and

microwaving it on full power for five minutes, depending on the size (make sure there are no metal parts on the jar). Empty, and allow to cool. Low, wide-necked jars are preferable so that the honey can be more easily removed. Once the honey has been poured into the jars they should be carefully sealed to prevent moisture absorption, which may cause fermentation, then labelled and dated. Attractive labels may be

purchased for a more professional look. Unless you produce honey on an industrial scale, using bees that have been restricted to specific flowers (such as heather), it is unlikely you will be able to identify the type of flower from which it came, for during the course of a season the bees will have collected nectar and pollen from all manner of flowering plants. This will be very evident once the honey extraction

process is begun; the colour of the honey may vary considerably, reflecting the shades and colours of the flower products from which it originated.

Having such a high sugar content, and being a natural antibacterial and antifungal, honey is considered a low-risk food. The above method is primarily intended for use at home when preparing honey for your own personal use. Some bee-keepers sell honey only occasionally in small and variable amounts according to the size of the harvest and the honey that is surplus to their requirements each year. Others, with a greater number of hives, may regard their bee-keeping as a sideline to earn extra money and may be supplying various retail outlets on a regular basis.

Remember that the rules are rather more stringent for bee-keepers supplying honey for sale to the public. In the United States, the Federal Food and Drug Administration or US Department of Agriculture should first be approached, while in England HM Government's requirements covering production, labelling and lot numbering should be consulted (see internet). (Other parts of Britain have their own statutory requirements.)

BACKYARD FARMING

Statutory regulations change from time to time, and your local Environmental Health Officer should also be approached for advice. Advisory leaflet No. 103: *So You Wish To Sell Honey*, also attempts to set out and clarify these requirements, and may be obtained from: BBKA The Bee Centre, National Agricultural Centre, Stoneleigh, Warwickshire, CV8.

Honey consists of fructose, glucose, water and other sugars. It also has many of the enzymes, vitamins, minerals and amino acids that your body needs to maintain health. It contains antioxidants that are used by the body to eliminate free radicals, which are the uncharged molecules which invade healthy cells and have the potential to damage them.

approved as an agent to help combat the dangerous MRSA bacteria, and it is also used in the treatment of diabetic ulcers. The antioxidants present in honey have also been attributed to the alleviation of conditions such as colitis, which is an inflammation of the colon.

Patients, after their tonsils are removed, are often prescribed honey, and indeed honey has been used for centuries to relieve sore throats and coughs, either taken in liquid form or in the form of honey lozenges. A particularly effective remedy to ease sore throats and relieve the affects of colds and flu can be achieved by sipping a mixture of two teaspoonfuls of honey with the juice of half a lemon from a cup topped up with boiling water. Adults may find this drink even more beneficial if a small tot of whisky is also added, especially at bedtime!

Cookery books are packed with recipes using honey; indeed, many of them are devoted solely to the art of cooking with this ingredient. Honey adds sweetness, body, a unique flavour and a delicious glaze to many dishes, and goes especially well with meats such as pork (and ham), chicken and duck, as well as with fish such as salmon. Food can be coated with

USES OF HONEY

This may seem an obvious and unnecessary section to include. After all, honey is for eating isn't it? Well, yes, of course it is, but honey has more to offer than simply being a form of food. Historically, it has been used as a trading commodity, as a natural preservative and as the basis for the alcoholic drink known as mead, but honey also plays a large role in medicine. For 2,700 years, and maybe even longer, humans have used honey to treat all manner of ailments, applying it to wounds, for example, to combat infection and speed the healing process, although it is only fairly recently that the antiseptic and antibacterial properties of honey have been fully explored. Honey is now honey, or it can be one of the ingredients of a marinade or sauce for meat or vegetables. It is often used to top waffles, fruit salads, breakfast cereals and yoghurts, or as a spread on bread or toast.

Apart from its use in making mead, of which there are numerous varieties, honey can be used in several other types of drinks, including mulled wines.

OTHER BEE PRODUCTS

Another useful commodity extracted from bees is the substance known as royal jelly, which is a secretion produced by the hypopharyngeal glands of worker bees and fed to developing larvae. Royal jelly is produced commercially by stimulating the colony to produce queen bees, from which the royal jelly is collected when the larvae are only a few days old. It is practical only to collect the royal jelly from developing queens, for although other larvae are also fed the substance for a few days, only queens receive a store of it that can be collected. During the processing of royal jelly, honey and

OPPOSITE & RIGHT: Honey and its byproducts have proven their worth over the centuries.

Beeswax is another natural product, secreted from special glands on the abdomens of worker bees. The wax is used for building the comb cells in which the young are raised and the pollen and honey stored. Beeswax is also variously used around hives to fill in gaps. During the honey extraction process (see page 188), the wax

beeswax are also added to help in its preservation.

Royal jelly is sold as a dietary supplement, and it is claimed to have various health benefits, due mainly to its high vitamin content, especially the B-complex. Royal jelly may also have some value in boosting the immune system, in the stimulation of stem cells in the brain, in lowering cholesterol, and as an antibiotic and anti-inflammatory – properties that are unlikely to be fulfilled if the product is ingested, when they are neutralized. Royal jelly is also a component of some beauty products.

cappings are cut from the comb. The colour of the wax varies according to the types of flowers on which the bees were feeding, but it is generally yellow, although it can vary from nearly white to brown. The wax is sieved off and gathered during the honey extraction process to be purified before being put to a variety of uses. As well as the many historical uses of beeswax, which included the making of candles, seals and sculptures, clarified beeswax is still used for candle-making today, as a lubricant in the woodworking and cabinet-making trade, for the smooth operation of drawers and windows, and in wood and shoe polishes when dissolved in turpentine.

Beeswax is occasionally used as a coating for cheeses and in the cosmetics industry (for example, as hair pomade), and is used in medicine to make dentistry casts and barrier creams, the cosmetics and pharmaceutical industries accounting for more than 50 per cent of the total consumption. It is

quite possible for bee-keepers to collect and refine beeswax for use in some of the aforementioned, and there are many books and websites that explain in detail exactly how this may be achieved.

Beeswax has been used in candle-making for thousands of years, and the candles made from it burn cleanly and emit the characteristic soft light and delicious aroma of warm honey.

CHAPTER SEVEN
KEEPING CHICKENS

We are looking here at what it's like to keep a single chicken, perhaps two, as a pet either for a child or even as a companion for a grown-up. We will also look at the pros and cons of keeping a small flock of chickens as a way of having your own supply of fresh eggs or even meat. Here, some of what is said about keeping a single chicken applies equally to keeping a flock, while much of the advice on feeding and general care is also appropriate to both.

First of all, and this applies to one chicken or several, the keeping of chickens is not permitted everywhere, so it may be best to check first with

RIGHT: Chickens make good pets for children, provided they have been taught to handle them correctly.

OPPOSITE: Many enjoy seeing their chickens pecking about in their backyards, and a colourful rooster is a particularly fine sight.

some individual chickens are tamer than others, even within a breed which is generally known to be well-disposed towards human beings. And it is certainly true that some breeds make better pets than others.

On the whole, breeds suitable for this purpose are those that are relatively light in weight (large chickens are difficult to pick up, especially by children). It is also sensible to choose a fairly hardy type and one that has no fancy or elaborate feathering, especially around the feet, since they are liable to cause problems in some cases if they are neglected. Bantams (usually smaller versions of 'standard' breeds, although sometimes breeds in their own right) can often be a good choice. Avoid male birds, since they can be aggressive by

your local authority. In any case there are liable to be some restrictions, and you will most likely find that your chicken or chickens won't be allowed to range free but must be kept in a suitable enclosure; there may also be some kind of ruling as to how close to human dwellings such a structure may be sited.

PET CHICKENS

Chickens have been kept as pets for centuries, and choosing the right one for the purpose often yields a surprisingly interesting and friendly companion. As with most other types of living things, nature. Some chicken breeds live longer than others, and this may also need to be taken into account.

Like many other kinds of animals, including other bird species, individual chickens each have their own traits and characteristics – let's call it their personality – and these features will become apparent as you study and get

to know your pet. If handled kindly from an early age, chickens can become quite affectionate, and one hen we know had the habit of coming up and resting her head on her owner's leg, as if asking for her head to be stroked.

Another aspect of keeping chickens is that many highly ornamental varieties now exist, with

features such as unusual coloration, feathering, and so on. In the event of choosing such a bird, showing them can be an interesting and rewarding pastime, and visiting exhibitions and shows can open up a whole new field of interest. But remember that some ornamental breeds may be less hardy and require more care to keep them in peak condition than other breeds.

As pets, chickens can be thought of as being reasonably 'low maintenance', which doesn't mean they should in any

and safe places in which to roost at night, and somewhere where they can shelter from the heat of the sun or from inclement weather during the day. Given suitable conditions and the right food, chickens will thrive, but their health will soon begin to suffer if they are neglected.

One of the greatest hazards facing chickens in a domestic setting is that of predators, and other pet animals, such as cats and dogs, will certainly take their toll given the chance. Wild animals such as foxes, squirrels,

way be treated in a cavalier fashion in terms of their welfare. Some chickens are hardier than others, as already mentioned, but they all need warm, dry

OPPOSITE LEFT & THIS PAGE RIGHT: Free-range chickens like nothing better than to be given the run of a garden, where they can peck around in their search for insects that may be incidentally harmful to existing plants.

OPPOSITE RIGHT: There are many varieties of pedigree chickens, all with different characteristics. This is a Silkie hen.

ABOVE: Chicken feeders allow just enough food through, keeping the remainder dry and rodent-free.

more opportunist, being commonly seen by day in many places, so keeping chickens securely fenced at all times is good practice, particularly if they are allowed to range free.

Rats and other rodents are also a problem in that they are attracted to places where there is a generous supply of spilled food, and beneath a chicken roost would be the ideal place for a rat or mouse family to set up home. One of the biggest threats is Weil's disease, which is carried in the rat's urine and can enter the human body through cuts and can also contaminate water. If left untreated the disease can be fatal, which is one reason why gloves should always be worn when cleaning out chickens. If you suspect rats are around – and you may even see them as they can be quite bold on occasions – put

LEFT: A traditional little brown hen. Chickens aren't the best of flyers, so special care must be taken to ensure their safety from predators and from local cats and dogs.

OPPOSITE: Foxes are probably the greatest predators and will go to great lengths to get to your chickens. Steps must therefore be taken to protect them at all times, and particularly at night.

raccoons and other prowling creatures are a real threat, and extremely upsetting though this may be, a fox will do more than kill a single chicken, and is liable to devastate an entire flock once it gets into an enclosure. Once considered more or less nocturnal, foxes of late have become bolder and down some poison or traps or, better still, get professionals in to deal with the problem. It goes without saying that any such measures must be implemented with due regard to the safety of children, pets, and the chickens themselves.

A Secure Place for Chickens

Many types of proprietary chicken housing systems are available, and there are plenty of companies around which can supply the items or even design and erect 'bespoke' housing especially for you. Have a look on the internet. In appearance, many typical proprietary systems are fairly similar to the type of structure often used for accommodating pet rabbits or guinea pigs outside. They are constructed of a wooden frame, which may be square or rectangular, usually with a side door for access. Other types may be triangular in cross-section, but in all cases the base of the run or pen is open to allow the birds to scratch and forage in the soil. One end of the pen includes the roost, which is a solid structure with a secure door and a waterproof top.

Unless you intend to let your chickens range freely, then an alternative system that works well is to

Good poultry houses protect chickens from the elements, injury and theft, and must also provide a stable environment in which the birds can feel comfortable during the day and at night, are protected against potential predators, and are provided with secure nesting boxes.

keep them in a large, strongly-made and permanently-sited pen – usually made from wire mesh attached to a wooden frame – and to include within it, or as part of it, a sturdy, solid-sided but well-ventilated roosting place. The outer pen must have sufficiently high sides to prevent the chickens from escaping, and if possible be high enough to discourage cats and other animals from getting in too easily; 5ft (1.6m) is the minimum for an open-topped run. A safer method is to have a relatively high-sided pen, with mesh covering the top as well, making it completely secure. Such an enclosed system is regularly used by keepers of cagebirds that are housed outside. But in the end, the best way to deter marauding foxes is to install electric fencing or electrified netting.

Once erected, although the fencing around the pen may seem in good order, check it regularly for signs of holes along the bottom; foxes may be trying to dig beneath the fencing to get in – a common and effective method used by them when trying to get into suburban gardens. It is best to ensure the bottom of the fencing extends a reasonable distance below ground (about 12in/30cm) to deter burrowing. Also, make sure the gauge of the mesh is correct – if the holes are too large a chicken may get its head caught while trying to peck at something outside. Holes that are too large will also allow the opportunist paws of a would-be predator to grab an unsuspecting chicken; 0.5-in (about 13-mm) mesh is usually recommended. As a general rule, if you are to put your chickens in a covered run, with occasional access to the garden or some other free-range spot, a pen area of about 4ft² (0.4m²) per bird should be allowed, but if they are to be confined at all times, then allow more space per bird, in this case about 10ft² (0.9m²)

Any pen should obviously be positioned on suitable, well-drained ground. A roughly grassed area or one that has soil and a few bushes is ideal: the chickens will soon turn it into a suitable habitat by scratching around in the earth, pecking at the foliage, and generally making themselves at home.

Tree stumps or other suitable objects scattered around will give them something that they can fly or hop onto, and will add interest to the environment. Like many birds, chickens like dust-baths, which help to remove lice and other parasites and scours the feathers clean. Therefore, in at least a part of the run there should be an area where the chickens can dig themselves a dust hole. If no such area is available, then a suitable, low container should be provided, filled with a mixture of ashes, dry soil and sand.

Like the pen, the chicken house or roost can be purchased ready-made, or you can erect one yourself, and there are plenty of books and websites that provide instructions. A typical roost is set slightly off the ground with a short ramp leading to the access door. It should be dry, draft-free but well-ventilated. Make sure the roost is sited where there is shade, otherwise it may get uncomfortably hot inside during the summer months.

The floor of the roost should be covered with clean straw laid on a thin layer of dust-free wood shavings, about an inch or two deep, which are readily available from pet supply stores and which should be changed regularly. Keep an eye on the 'bedding' to check for droppings, which must be removed

everyday. A removable droppings tray, placed beneath the roosting poles, will help to ensure that everything is kept clean and healthy. The soiled bedding makes good compost, so nothing need be wasted.

The roost should be cleared out weekly and fresh bedding laid down. Then, at least twice a year, but more often if conditions seem to dictate, the roost should be thoroughly stripped out and deep-cleaned. Everything should be removed, including bedding, nest boxes and any feeding containers. A safe cleaning agent should then be used to disinfect the walls, floor, roosting poles, and so on. Rinse everything with fresh water and allow to dry thoroughly before letting the chickens return. Fresh, clean bedding should be laid on the floor of the roost and in the nest box.

Allow an area of 1.5ft^3 (0.04m^3) per bird in the enclosed space of a roost, and make sure that it is sturdily constructed with a strong base. Once the chickens are safely inside for the night, the access door to the coop should be shut securely with a bolt or a similar arrangement; if a predator, such

OPPOSITE: These chickens are living within a large, well-fenced pen where there is space for foraging and a place to which they can retreat at night.

RIGHT: An ideal night-time environment is a barn where there are plenty of high places where chickens can roost.

as a fox, should get into the outer pen, the roost must be sufficiently robust to prevent entry here as well. The small wooden pivoting bar, so often seen on the doors of animal houses, is not sufficient protection against a determined animal like a fox, which will inevitably knock the bar down when scratching to get in and thus allow the door to open.

Chickens, being birds, have a natural urge to roost off the ground at night for security, like others of their kind. Therefore roosting perches should be provided so that your chicken or chickens can rest snugly off the floor. Perches should be about 2in (5cm) wide for standard breeds but a little narrower for smaller birds. Allow 10in (25cm) across for the bird, and the same amount of space between roosting poles if you have more than one chicken. If you do install several perches, it is best to have them graded slightly in terms of level, so that the birds do not all roost at exactly the same height. An inch or two is sufficient; don't set them so high that the birds have difficulty getting up to them. Roosting perches should be constructed of timber that has had its bark removed, as cracks and spaces left by fragmenting bark may harbour undesirable insects.

As long as the roost is well-ventilated but free from drafts (this is especially important), there is normally no need to add heat to it in winter. Chickens will adapt to a falling temperature as the seasons change, and it is best that they should not be faced with the fluctuating temperatures that arise by going from a warm roost to a cold outside run. Problems may also arise if, at any time, the power was to fail in a heated roost, and birds that have been accustomed to warm conditions at night may even die as a result.

FOOD AND WATER

Fresh drinking water must be available at all times when the chickens are in the pen. Under normal circumstances it is not necessary to provide water for them in the coop or roost as long as the birds are let out into the pen each morning to access drinking water for themselves. Various types of water dispensers are available, such as fountains which automatically fill up a trough with fresh water. Whatever type of water supply is used, ensure it is fixed at the recommended height and in accordance with the supplier's instructions. Don't use a water dispenser that might be fouled by the chickens hopping onto it. In cold weather, make sure that the water supply, or the reservoir, if one is fitted, is not allowed to freeze; chickens won't be able to survive for long without water. To ensure it remains ice-free, water can be brought into a warm place overnight and returned to the run the next morning.

The wild relatives of the domestic chicken enjoy a varied diet, ranging

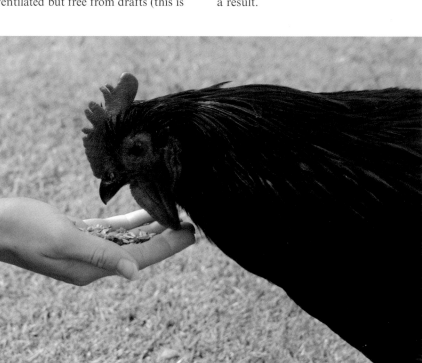

LEFT: Pet chickens often become tame enough to take food from the hand.

OPPOSITE: Suitable feeding methods.

from seeds and other vegetation to insects and even small lizards. Domestic chickens are also omnivorous in their feeding habits, and have even been known to catch and devour the odd mouse that gets into the enclosure! However, for those new to keeping chickens, it is advisable to base the feeding regime around one of the good-quality proprietary complete pellet feeds that are available; this will ensure they get a balanced diet of carbohydrate, fat and protein, vitamins and minerals (such as calcium needed for eggshells). Use a commercially

supplied dispenser or hopper for the pellets to stop them getting wet. A little grain can also be added, such as wheat or corn, to augment the diet if preferred, which can be scattered around the pen area; most authorities advise this should be offered in the afternoon, with the pellet food being given in the morning.

Grit is essential for many birds, not only chickens. Because they are without teeth, the abrasive properties of grit are needed in their crops (part of the digestive system) to help them grind up their food. Some grit should be present in good-quality proprietary feed, but it

LEFT: Collecting fresh eggs for the table is an appealing thought.

BELOW: Broody hens need stress-free environments and clean and comfortable conditions if they are to incubate their eggs so that hatching of the chicks can take place.

OPPOSITE: A pedigree hen and her chicks. These exotic types are more often kept for showing rather than as pets.

should be lower than the highest roosting pole, however. Position the nest box in a quiet, dark place to help her feel more secure. Again, there is

is worth providing a small container with an extra supply so that the chickens can take as much as they need.

Chickens also appreciate a little fresh greenery, so let them get onto grass as often as is possible, or offer them plants to eat such as chickweed. Chickens are also happy to eat leftovers from the kitchen, but not of course as a substitute for properly designed chicken feed. They will eat fruit, cabbage, vegetable peelings, and so on. Do not, however, offer them anything strong-tasting such as onion, garlic or spices; neither should they be given citrus

fruits (such as oranges and lemons) nor any food in the process of 'going off'. Chickens shouldn't eat rotten food any more than we should ourselves; moreover, the likelihood is that it will be rejected and will be left to rot still further, eventually attracting vermin and flies.

EGG-LAYING

Even if you are keeping a single hen as a pet, she will reward you with eggs if you encourage her to lay. A nest box should be provided, raised a few inches off the ground within the roost; it

plenty of advice available in books and on the internet about how to create the ideal conditions for successful egg-laying. For example, it is possible to buy dummy eggs made from stone that encourage first layers to sit on their eggs without crushing them. (When young, I used to have great fun dropping these eggs in front of people, who didn't realize they were not real, just to see the shocked expression on their faces!)

The bottom of the nest should be lined with a little clean straw or pinewood shavings to help prevent the eggs from breaking when they are laid. (Despite all these measures, you will inevitably find broken eggs in the roost

211

from time to time.) Contrary to popular belief, a chicken will still lay eggs whether a cockerel is present or not. The only difference is that without a cockerel around to fertilize them they will never produce chicks.

OBTAINING CHICKENS

Once all the necessary accommodation and equipment is in place you can begin to think about obtaining birds and introducing them to their new home. At this point it is more than likely that you have made a decision concerning the type of chicken you want and why you want it; in other words, will it be essentially for eggs or for eating, will it be for showing or simply to be kept as a pet? You will need to consider the different types of chickens, their suitability from your point of view, their size, colour, temperament and hardiness. The more you can find out beforehand from other sources, including breeders and the internet, the better. Seeing the actual breed in the flesh, moreover, is the best way of ensuring you will ultimately be satisfied with your choice.

If you wish to keep chickens primarily for the quality of their eggs, then a commercial hybrid is the best

choice. If you would prefer the eggs to be of a particular colour, then go for a pure breed. Wyandottes and Rhode Island Reds, for example, are among the breeds that lay mid-brown eggs, Leghorns lay white eggs, and Sussex hens tinted eggs, while Welsummers

and Barnevelders lay dark-brown eggs, and those of Araucanas are blue. One of the drawbacks with hybrids is that they do not have the distinctive look of some of the more spectacular breeds, but in their favour is the fact that they are cheaper to buy, come vaccinated against disease, and are excellent layers, some producing well in excess of 300 eggs in a year. Hybrids, of course, are the mainstay of the commercial industry for both meat and eggs.

Most breeds have their own clubs, whose members can put you in touch with reputable local breeders in your area who can sell you a pullet (a young hen under a year old). It is always best to visit the premises of the breeder from whom you intend to buy, so that you can assess the conditions under which the birds have been raised. Talk to the breeder and explain your reasons for wanting the breed you have chosen and try to obtain as much information

It is fortunate for those of us who enjoy her eggs that hens, given a little care and encouragement, are able to continue laying even when no rooster is present in the flock. A male will be needed, however, if the eggs are to be made fertile and eventually hatch to produce chicks.

as you can: how to care for it, any special traits it may have, and so on. Becoming a member of the breed club for the chickens you have chosen is a good way of obtaining more information. Another way, before making a purchase, is to visit a poultry show or an event such as a country fair, where various breeds can be viewed.

Another route is to buy fertilized eggs and place them in an incubator until they hatch. This is particularly exciting for children, and there is the added benefit of seeing the chick at the very earliest stages in its life. If you are planning to try this, you must ensure that all the necessary equipment is in place before you obtain the eggs. There are plenty of books and websites that tell you how to set up an incubator, what the correct temperature should be, and what to do once the chicks have hatched (for example, they need to be fed on chick starter feed for about six weeks, followed by a pullet feed). It is likely that most sources of information will also warn you to make sure that the chicks are kept safe from another form of predator – in this case the pet cat or dog – which may be tempted to eat a small chick sitting in a warm box in the house!

KEEPING CHICKENS

LEFT: Some breeds of chicken are more amenable than others and make better pets where children are concerned.

OPPOSITE: Choose your chicken according to the purpose for which it is required, either for the fact that it is an excellent egg-layer, it produces tasty meat, or it has the friendly disposition that will make it an ideal pet.

Ex-battery hens, which have reached the end of their commercial life – usually at about 72 weeks – are fast becoming another choice for the amateur chicken-keeper or for those who want a bird or a number of birds that they can keep on a small scale. There are several organizations that specialize in rescuing these hens and offering them to people willing to give them a new life. It can be an initially sad yet ultimately rewarding experience to take on one of these birds. Some of them will be traumatized and even in bad condition to begin with; they may have poor feathering, and may even need to regrow their beaks. But just as with other rescue animals, such as cats and dogs, with the proper care and attention there is no reason why they should not, in time, return to their full vigour and fine appearance.

How To Handle a Chicken

As with most animals, there is a right and a wrong way to pick up a chicken, for one that is dropped or mishandled, though unintentionally, is likely to become wary and apprehensive even of being stroked, and won't make a good pet as a result. For this reason, it is advisable that young children are taught the correct way to handle a chicken right from the start. Remember that large breeds don't always make good pets; the urge to pick up and cuddle is enormously strong in children, but large animals don't fit into small arms!

Before you pick up a chicken, it is often useful to let it get to know you first. Try offering a few tasty morsels, or approach very slowly and attempt to touch or stroke the bird. First place your dominant hand (the one you write with) on the middle of the chicken's back. Use the thumb and forefinger of that hand to gently but firmly secure the wings so that they can't flap. Now, using your other hand, enclose one of the chicken's legs with your thumb and forefinger, and the other with the forefinger and middle finger of the same hand. Now lift the chicken up, using the heel of your hand and your wrist to support the underside, keeping your dominant hand on the chicken's back in the meantime. Now you can hold the chicken close to your body to prevent it from wriggling; it's best to sit down with the chicken at this point. After a time, the chicken will come to realize that this activity on your part results in its movements being somewhat curtailed, and as time goes on it should cease to struggle. Soon you should be able to pick it up without any fuss, especially if you talk to the bird gently and stroke it while it is in your arms.

KEEPING CHICKENS HEALTHY

Chickens are pretty robust and healthy most of the time, but they can succumb to illness and disease like any other animal. Chickens kept in flocks can quickly transmit diseases to others, which will compound the initial problem. If detected early enough, however, most ailments can be treated. Before this happens, however, it is

worth acquainting yourself with details of a vet in your area who is skilled in avian (bird) medicine. Ask your local vet if he can provide such a service, and if not, ask him to recommend another who can. Your local authority or pet rescue centre may also be able to offer advice, since they may themselves call upon veterinary services from time to time. Symptoms of disease can manifest themselves in various ways, so it is sensible to check each chicken daily to

ensure they are not presenting any early signs. Look in particular for the following:

• Listlessness or loss of appetite – does the chicken seem to be behaving differently from normal?

• Poor feather condition – feathers should appear sleek and 'well-groomed' in a healthy bird. Do not confuse poor feather condition with moulting, which all birds undergo to replace their feathers as part of the natural cycle.

Egg-laying will also be curtailed during the moulting period.

• Any obvious change in the pecking order; if you have more than one chicken, is the one in question being bullied or dominated by one normally lower in rank?

• Sneezing.

• Parasites on the feathers or skin, or a generally 'mangy' appearance.

• Unusual-looking stools (droppings) and/or the appearance in the stools of worms; normal stools are brownish with a white 'cap'.

It must be stressed, however, that these are not the only signs of illness, and if you have any other reasons to suspect that not all is well, expert advice should be sought as soon as possible.

Many diseases may be brought about by poor hygiene regimes in the coop, so make sure that the cleaning procedures described earlier are followed at all times.

In addition to dealing with illnesses, there are a number of measures that should be taken to

ensure your chickens remain healthy. These include preventing worms or dealing with them once they are detected. There are several types of parasitic worm, of which the most common is the roundworm. Chickens afflicted with these can suffer weight loss, feather-fluffing, diarrhoea, and in severe cases even death. Boggy ground, that attracts earthworms (one of the carriers of roundworms), can be a cause of the problem.

Tapeworms are less commonly problematical but are still a cause for concern, and similar symptoms as those shown by roundworm infestation are often seen. In cases of worm infestation, or to prevent worms, an anti-worming treatment is advised. This should be carried out at least twice-yearly, or according to your vet's instructions. During the treatment, and for a period following it, none of the affected chicken's eggs should be consumed.

The beaks of birds grow continually, as do our own fingernails, this constant growth being an important factor that repairs normal wear and tear. Chickens that range freely tend to keep their own beaks in trim through the abrasive action of

pecking around in the soil. However, it is possible that the upper mandible (the top part of the beak) will sometimes overgrow the lower one if the chicken is not allowed to feed in this manner – for example, if the food is too soft and the conditions for general pecking and foraging are not met. If the beak does overgrow in this way, it must be trimmed back, otherwise the chicken will not be able to eat and drink normally. Experienced chicken-keepers often do this job themselves, but initially it is advisable to have a vet or similarly qualified person do it for you so that you may see for yourself how it is done.

Claws may also need trimming, since they grow in the same way as the beak. Again, in ideal conditions, all the scratching at the ground, which a chicken does in the normal course of finding food, will tend to keep the claws at the correct length; but if they get too long – usually as a result of

OPPOSITE ABOVE: Choose a bird that is very tame, then use it to teach your child the correct way to pick up and hold a chicken.

RIGHT: Check your chickens regularly for signs and symptoms of disease.

walking on soft litter – then they will need to be cut back, otherwise foot problems can ensue. Like the beak, this is a job you can do yourself, but to begin with, a 'lesson' from an experienced person is required.

Some chickens are born with beak defects, such as one that is twisted to

the left or right instead of growing straight. There may also be a visible gap between the upper and lower mandibles when the mouth is closed. Such conditions can affect the bird's ability to eat properly, and special foods may be required. Unless caused by an injury, defects of this type are normally genetic in origin, and if you intend to breed your chickens it is best not to use such birds in order to avoid passing the condition onto the next generation.

External parasites, such as lice and mites, can also be a problem. Lice are

To avoid disease, keep coops clean and disinfected and regularly change soiled bedding material.

easier to spot than mites, since they are bigger; they may be seen around the bases of the feathers and their eggs may be seen visibly attached to them. Look particularly around the vent and under the wings where the softer downy feathers grow. Dust baths help chickens get rid of lice naturally, but special treatments are also available to rid them of these troublesome parasites.

There are several types of mite: red mites do not actually live on the chicken, but lurk in crevices in the roost. At night, when the chickens are resting on their perches, the mites come out to feed on the hosts' blood. The irritation they cause can make the chickens pluck out their own feathers or desert their nests if brooding, so a complete eradication programme is needed to deal with the problem.

As well as treating the birds, the infestation must be removed from every likely place in the roost by washing (preferably with water under high pressure) and then treating all surfaces, including perches, with a poultry-safe disinfectant. Another type of mite infesting chickens is known as the northern fowl mite, and the bird should be treated to eradicate these.

Another mite-related condition is scaly leg, which is often brought about by keeping birds in damp living conditions. The mites burrow into the scales on the chickens' legs, which then become inflamed and painful. If left untreated, the mites' excreta builds up and causes the scales to lift away from the legs, in which case your vet should be asked to deal with the problem.

Various other diseases may be encountered, such as coccidiosis, which is a minute single-celled parasite. It is usually present in low levels in chickens (chicks acquire a measure of immunity to the parasite through exposure as they develop), but poor housing conditions, such as overcrowding and lack of ventilation, can exacerbate the condition. Young chickens from about three to six weeks old are most susceptible to the disease, but older birds can also suffer. Giving the chicks a feed containing an anti-coccidial agent will help to reduce the risk.

Mycoplasma is a respiratory disease affecting birds, usually those that have already been weakened by a virus, since the condition is often already present in them in low concentrations. Marek's disease is a virus that often affects domestic chickens, although it is rarer in commercial stock since they are inoculated against the disease when they are a day old. Particularly susceptible are Silkies and Sebrights.

A compacted crop is a common problem with chickens. As we saw earlier, the crop is part of the bird's digestive system, in which food taken by the mouth is stored before passing to the gizzard, where it is ground up prior to being digested. Somehow, the food in the crop does not always pass down to the gizzard and instead becomes blocked, with indigestion, obstruction or ill-health being the main reasons. Offer the chicken some warm water to drink while at the same time rubbing the crop gently with your hand to loosen the compacted material. Then, holding the chicken with its head held slightly downward, gently squeeze the crop, which should force the liquid to run out. Now offer more water and then prevent the chicken from feeding for 24 hours. Again, this technique is one that is best done after having watched someone perform it first.

One of the conditions that often afflicts chickens kept as pets is obesity, brought about by the same reasons that cause the problem in humans, i.e., too much food, and of the wrong type, and not enough exercise. Chickens are a little like some breeds of dog in their eating habits, tending to wolf down whatever they are given, especially if they are kitchen scraps. Poor egg-laying and infertility are just two of the problems connected with an overweight chicken. To check for obesity, feel for the breastbone; it should be possible to detect it beneath a reasonable layer of fat. If the breastbone feels sharp, it is likely that the chicken is in fact underweight, but if it is difficult to feel it at all, then the likelihood is that the bird is carrying too much weight.

To avoid overfeeding, make sure no food remains by the time the bird is ready to roost, but if there is food left over, try cutting it back a little. As a rough guide, each adult bird should receive about 4oz (113g) of food per day, given that they may well supplement this amount with extra food obtained from foraging.

NEW ARRIVALS AND THE PECKING ORDER

Once you have a few chickens you may decide to add more to your flock, and this is a process that needs to be handled in the right way. We have already seen that chickens live according to a hierarchical system, known as a pecking order, and healthy chickens will live quite happily under this self-imposed regime once it has become established. Once newcomers are introduced into this nice and tidy arrangement, however, the whole system is temporarily thrown into confusion, and the birds will need to re-establish their relative places within the flock. Things will usually settle down again within a week or so, but in the meantime much quarrelling, bullying, and general unpleasantness is likely to ensue. There are things you can do, however, to alleviate the turmoil to some extent.

The bullying of newcomers will be more severe if the existing chickens have little to do, but if they can be distracted from this activity so much the better. Introducing some additional features into the run, such as a few large tree branches with twigs, will give the newcomers somewhere to hide or escape the attention of the aggressors, while providing extra food sources, such a grass cuttings, dead leaves, some weeds or some kitchen scraps, will also give the hens something more interesting on which to focus their attentions. Hanging a cabbage just out of their reach will also give them something else on which to concentrate. If possible, letting the chickens out to range freely is another good way of reducing the tension, allowing them to become accustomed to the newcomers while they concentrate on foraging. Do not allow the newcomers out to range freely for a few days until they have recognized that the run and the coop are their new home.

Should your chickens develop bare patches of skin throughout the year, it is likely they are pecking one another – usually a sign that they are under stress. Since contented chickens do not usually indulge in this behaviour, it is important to investigate the source of the stress so that it can be removed. But beware that in the worst cases, a chicken may even resort to eating another.

Check there is sufficient space (see pages 204 et seq.) in the run and in the roost. Are the chickens competing for too few feeders or water containers? Are there enough nest boxes and roosts to go around, and are they positioned sufficiently distant from one another? Are the chickens infested with parasites? If none of these factors appears to be the cause of the problem, then it is advisable to consult your vet, so that he can make his diagnosis and suggest solutions.

The pecking order will need to be re-established when adding further chickens to an existing flock. This is facilitated by providing added distractions and eliminating overcrowding.

CHAPTER EIGHT
KEEPING LIVESTOCK

This chapter must be treated only as very general advice for those thinking of keeping livestock, and far more detailed instruction and advice must be obtained before this can be put into action. The slaughter and butchery of animals for food is not covered here; this is a specialist procedure, and must be carried out by experts according to the local government regulations and guidelines current at the time.

PIGS

Pigs (hogs) are often near to the top of the list when it comes to keeping free-range livestock on a small scale. Pigs will eat almost anything they are given, and can even digest grass, though they will not thrive on this alone. They will also convert virtually everything you grow yourself into the most delicious meat and byproducts. And while they may not be everyone's idea of the perfect pet, the fact that they are such pleasant, cheerful and intelligent creatures makes them a pleasure to have around.

BEFORE STARTING

Rushing headlong into pig ownership, without considering all the implications, is a recipe for disaster Pigs need to be housed properly and

OPPOSITE: Your land must be carefully rersearched, even before contemplating keeping livestock, to see if it is suitable and able to support the number of animals you have in mind.

RIGHT: Piglets are enchanting and difficult to resist, but remember that they will inevitably grow up and may live for more than 20 years.

are becoming increasingly available. These offer fun introductions to the subject, allowing you to handle the animals while gathering valuable information and advice. They will also help you get to grips with the paperwork and legal side of keeping pigs. You must also check government guidelines and legislation, much of which needs sorting out even before you buy your pigs, and which must be followed whether you have just one pig or several.

MAKING A CHOICE

Some will opt for one of the rarer breeds, not only with the idea of protecting them from extinction, but

they need space to run around. They will also plough up your land, and may even eat you out of house and home. Remember that even though they may start out small and adorable, they will grow to be very large indeed. Like all animals, pigs can get sick and die and, if not used for meat, may live for 20 years, making them very long-term commitments.

You would be well-advised to enrol yourself in one of the many excellent courses on pig-keeping that

also because they produce tastier meat. Popular American breeds to consider are: Duroc, American Landrace and Yorkshire, while others include Berkshire, British Lop, British Saddleback, Gloucestershire Old Spot, Large Black, Middle White, Tamworth and Welsh. The American Livestock Breed Conservancy and the British Rare Breeds Survival Trust are excellent sources of information.

Each breed has its own characteristics and it is important to match it to the type of land on which it will live. It may also be worthwhile seeking out others who keep pigs in your area, in the hope that their intimate knowledge of a particular breed might prove to be of interest and particular value to you.

BUYING PIGS

The important thing, when acquiring pigs, is to make sure they come from a reputable breeder, and the various

Rare-breed pigs dislike being herded together in factory conditions, and prefer the open air, where they can grow more slowly. Not only do they have happier lives, but they also produce meat with superior eating qualities.

associations and societies, that concern themselves with particular breeds, will advise you accordingly.

Keeping pigs outdoors presents a number of problems, including 'heat stress', because they have no sweat glands to naturally cool themselves. Therefore pigs require access to water or a 'wallow', which is an area of mud, otherwise they will roll in their own excrement, which they would not normally do. Ideally, a cement wallow, which contains water, cools the pigs much better, although mud serves to protect light-coloured pigs from sunburn. It is also important that shade is provided. Remember that pigs are rooting animals and voracious feeders, and will strip every plant in their vicinity. They will soon make a 'mess' of their pen, which belies the fact that they are actually clean animals.

ABOVE & OPPOSITE RIGHT: Pigs must be given a dry area off the ground, with plenty of clean bedding to lie on, where they can shelter from the weather.

OPPOSITE LEFT: Pigs, because they have no sweat glands, need to cool themselves another way by wallowing in mud.

HOUSING

Somewhere will also be needed to accommodate them. Pig arks are suitable for this purpose and are readily available, these being triangular structures raised off the ground to ensure the animals remain dry. The pigs will need plenty of straw, and some form of fencing to keep them on their own patch and out of yours. Electric fencing works well for this purpose, but wooden post-and-rail is easier on the eye if the pen is to be in full view of your house.

FEEDING

Pigs are non-ruminants with a single stomach, unlike such animals as cattle and goats. To grow rapidly and efficiently, they need a high-energy, concentrated grain diet that is low in fibre (cellulose) and is supplemented with adequate protein.

One-half to two-thirds of a pig's body is made up of water, making it the most important part of its diet. Therefore it should be supplied with as much clean, fresh water as it will drink. Be careful not to overfeed your

animals and, while giving them scraps from the kitchen and garden is a good idea, do not feed them meat, which is illegal in many countries.

HEALTH

Remember that not all vets will accept pigs as patients, so it's worth checking this out in the early stages and not waiting for an emergency to strike. Pigs tend to stay relatively fit, because of the foraging they do, but it is worth getting them used to being stroked and handled, which will make life easier should they need to be examined by a vet. It will also make keeping pigs that bit more enjoyable for you.

COWS

Cattle occupy a unique role in human history, having been domesticated since at least the early Neolithic period. Cattle are ruminants, meaning they have a digestive system that allows otherwise indigestible food to be consumed, by repeatedly regurgitating and rechewing it as 'cud'. Cattle are raised for meat (beef cattle), dairy products and hides.

Keeping livestock of any kind is a big responsibility and should never be taken lightly. Before getting a cow of your own, consider borrowing one for a week or so to see what is involved and how it will affect your own daily routine.

There are many benefits to keeping a cow, the main one being that a daily supply of fresh, unpasteurised milk and cream will be readily available to turn into your own butter and cheese. A little additional income can also be generated from the produce.

You will need to feed and milk your cow every morning and night, at 12-hourly intervals. She will need to be mated with a bull once a year to make her pregnant, so that she keeps on producing milk. You will then need to raise the young calf and either keep it or sell it on at market.

Keeping a cow will also entail butter- and cheese-making, growing and harvesting hay and sugar beet to feed your cow, also grooming, cleaning and mucking out the barn.

OPPOSITE: To keep a cow, you will need at least an acre of pasture and a warm draft-free barn with good ventilation.

ABOVE: A Jersey calf. Jerseys make excellent dairy cows.

MAKING A CHOICE

Jersey cows are often the first choice because they are small and produce rich milk. They are also said to make good pets. Whatever the breed, it is a good idea to get the same breed as other farmers in your locality, so that when it comes to mating your cow there will be a suitable bull available.

BUYING COWS

When buying a cow, choose the healthiest one possible (you will need a vet to check her over). Make sure she has been tested for tuberculosis and check her udders for signs of mastitis. Examine milking records to ensure she produces a good yield.

Once the initial cost of buying a cow has been made, and all the necessary equipment bought, there should be very few other outgoings. By growing and harvesting your own hay, moreover, there will be little need to feed her with grain, which only leaves further outlay for possible veterinary treatment and the purchase of additional bedding for use during the winter months.

HOUSING & EQUIPMENT

Some basic equipment needs to be bought once the decision has been made. The first item to consider is a barn that will accommodate your cow in winter. It should be comfortable and draft-free and with a window to let in plenty of sunlight and fresh air. Storage will also be required for the bales of hay needed to feed her. Only a little space is needed if you decide to buy hay by the bale, but rather more storage will be required if you intend to produce your own hay.

It is important that the barn has its own supply of running water, both for the cow to drink and for cleaning purposes.

It is also worth keeping a three-bin compost system nearby, so that well-rotted manure is always available for use on your vegetable patch.

At least one acre of land is required per cow, divided into three separate pastures which the cow can graze in rotation and where you can grow and harvest your own hay.

General milking equipment will include a milk pail, water pail, milking stool, manure shovel and

ABOVE: It is a good idea, provided there is sufficient land, to produce enough hay to see your cow through the winter months.

OPPOSITE: In many countries, animals need to be registered and ears tagged.

fork, halter and rope, comb and brush, barn thermometer, udder washcloths, milk scale, hay forks and a wheelbarrow. You may also wish to invest in a milk churn, in which to make butter, as well as cheese-making equipment.

FEEDING & HEALTH
During the spring, summer and autumn months, cows return to the fields after milking. Grass is the cheapest form of food, and well-managed herds are able to produce lots of milk from it.

The most important consideration is to keep your cow, and her milk, healthy. Keep her out on pasture until the cold winter months, then give her all the quality hay she needs, to which may be added a half-pound or so of grain while milking, with a vitamin-

mineral supplement as extra insurance. Silage is also a valuable food; this is a form of pickling that preserves summer grass for use during the winter months. A salt block to lick on should also be provided, also plenty of fresh water.

Mastitis and lameness are the most common adverse conditions

Good feeding is all-important where health is concerned. Cows need a grassy paddock in the warmer months of the year and a warm barn and plenty of hay or silage in winter.

affecting cows, and if these or any other forms of disease are suspected, a vet must be called at once.

GOATS

Goats have had something of a bad reputation for centuries. Not only were they long associated with satanists and the devil, but we are also warned of their habit of springing an attack any time our backs are turned. But the reality is very different; in fact goats are charming animals with a great deal of character. According to the ancient Greeks, the Capricorn of the zodiac was sexy, lively and health-giving. The

females do not smell, if looked after properly, and the milk, besides tasting good, is easier to digest than cow's, can be tolerated by people with allergies, and makes excellent cheese.

Goats are in many ways the ideal choice for the smallholder, but they are not to be compared with sheep, being sociable and capable of forming complex relationships with others in their herd. For this reason, it would be unkind to keep one goat on its own.

MAKING A CHOICE
All females that have produced kids should give milk, but some breeds give more than others, and selection processes have resulted in a number of breeds that are kept largely for milk production; Swiss breeds are the most prolific where this is concerned. There are also breeds that are kept specifically for meat, such as the Boer, while others, such as the Turkish Angora, are kept for their hair.

OPPOSITE: Goats, being relatively small, are ideal for backyard farming, and are fairly easy to maintain. They also produce good milk and make charming pets.

RIGHT: A pygmy goat.

235

KEEPING LIVESTOCK

HOUSING

A dry, draft-free building is required, with shelter from the elements and sufficient headroom for an animal to stand upright on its hindlegs with neck outstretched. Good ventilation and natural lighting are essential, but all windows should be protected from goat damage. The floor area, where the goat lies down, must be draft-free in bad weather. If penned separately, each goat should have about 44ft^2 (4m^2) of floor space. Goats like to see one another, even if penned separately, so provision needs to be made to accommodate this.

BELOW & OPPOSITE: Goats, being hardy creatures, require minimal shade and shelter during summer and the occasional drizzle, but sturdier accommodation is needed in winter and for birthing and kidding.

A well-fenced exercise yard is needed at least three to four times the

area of the penning. This needs to be concreted or have a similar hard surface that does not retain moisture and that can be easily cleaned. Otherwise goats can be turned out to graze/browse in a well-fenced paddock during the day in all but very bad weather. Field shelters are appreciated.

Horned and disbudded or hornless goats should be penned separately.

A dry area is needed in which to store straw, hay and other feed. Protect it from damp, contamination and vermin. A nearby supply of fresh water is also required, as is a clean area for milking if you have a dairy goat.

FEEDING

Goats, left to their own devices, wander about taking a little of this and

something of that. They find hedgerows particularly attractive. Good hay is the single most important item of diet. At least half the diet (on a dry weight basis) should consist of forage. Green food, concentrates, minerals, vitamins and water are also important, and a balanced and adequate diet is crucial for good health. Any change to the diet must be made gradually to

enable the rumen bacteria to adjust. Other foods are a good quality goat mix and sugar beet pulp.

Individual pens need hayracks, feed and water buckets and bucket-holders. Feed and hay are usually placed outside pens, allowing the goats to feed through a slatted barrier. To prevent bullying, there should be a sufficient number of openings in the slats for all to feed at once. Salt licks should be provided at all times.

OPPOSITE & BELOW: Female goats are one of those rare animals that sometimes produce milk without being pregnant, although offspring are produced in the usual way, with help from a male; you will need to decide whether to keep the kids or sell them once they are born.

HEALTH

Good health can only be achieved as part of good management in general, including adequate housing, exercise and feeding, the prevention and treatment of parasitic worm infestations being particularly important.

Close observation of your goats is essential if you are to learn what is 'normal' and what is not. Since some Goats are very good climbers, therefore you will need to provide a high fence if you wish to keep them contained. Giving them something to climb onto, however, will keep them happy and active.

conditions have gradual onsets, being able to spot symptoms should enable you to act promptly and prevent risk to other goats in the vicinity.

Males may become sexually active when only a few weeks old, which means they must be kept separate from females from about six weeks of age to avoid accidents. Males are used for stud purposes in their first autumn, although late-born kids may not be ready until later in the breeding season.

ABOVE & RIGHT: Goats are active creatures, and pens must be big enough to accommodate their needs.

SHEEP

There are good reasons for keeping sheep: they provide fine fleeces, delicious meat and are great at cropping grass and keeping it short. But if you're planning on getting some yourself, then you'll need to be properly prepared.

Making a Choice

Different breeds of sheep thrive on different types of grazing, so speak to local farmers and discover which best suit the environment. Sheep have more breed types than any other farm animal, so there are plenty from which to choose.

BELOW & OPPOSITE: Many people enjoy keeping rare breeds, which is a good thing as it helps to prevent them from dying out. Their fleeces can also be quite valuable.

Lush pasture should accommodate around four to five sheep per acre, so plan numbers accordingly,

remembering that it is better to have too few than too many.

BUYING SHEEP

Once you've decided how many sheep (and which kind) you want, there are two main choices: either find a farmer who breeds sheep for sale, or head for market. If possible, a private purchase from a reputable breeder is the best option, in which case thc breeder will be able to give you valuable advice, and you can study the sheep in your own time in open fields. The sheeps' medical and family history can also be obtained at the same time.

Market purchases can be cheaper, but sheep bought in this manner come into contact with many others of their kind along the way, and disease can spread as a result.

To keep sheep on your own land, you'll need to obtain all the relevant paperwork. Legislation varies throughout the world and you may need to register your property as an 'agricultural holding'.

Record-keeping may also be mandatory, with regulations governing the movement of livestock adhered to at all times. For more information regarding the legalities of keeping sheep in Britain, visit the DEFRA website; in the USA, you should contact your local US Department of Food and Agriculture.

FEEDING
For most of the year sheep are

content with grass, weeds and water. Indeed, one of the reasons why they are so popular is that they help to keep fields from becoming overgrown. In winter, however, when the ground is frost-hardened and the grass is short of nutrients, it will be necessary to supplement their diet with hay and grain.

If you have only a few sheep, give them a handful of 'sheep nuts' from a bucket each day. This routine helps to train the sheep, eventually allowing you to manoeuvre them without help from a sheepdog.

OPPOSITE & BELOW: Lush pasture should support four to five sheep per acre.

HEALTH

Of all livestock, sheep are probably the most susceptible to infections and infestations that can either affect productivity or kill them. The existence of insect vectors means that a clean environment is important; diseases can also be transmitted through faeces and from close contact with other infected animals.

Fortunately, sheep are fairly hardy, and diseases can be kept to a minimum if they are kept in good conditions, with well-ventilated housing and rotated between different areas of grass. Good hygiene starts with ensuring that hooves and wool are kept clear of faecal matter, in which flies and other insects are likely to lay their larvae, and which go on to eat into the flesh of the sheep. Diseases of the hooves include paratuberculosis and foot and mouth, when it is vital to separate affected animals from the rest of the herd. Sheep are also subject to scab, diarrhoea (scour), ticks, lice, fleas, orf, fly strike and pasteurella. Lameness and foot problems being fairly

Control disease by rotating pasture at intervals, maintaining clean living environments and checking stock regularly.

common, it is important to inspect feet regularly. It is also necessary to trim feet from time to time, depending on the terrain on which the sheep are kept.

Kept outside, sheep will naturally segregate the areas where they defecate and rest, and space should be allowed to accommodate this. Pens should be washed out every day, if necessary, and sheep should be given an antiseptic bath at least once a week. Netting pens will also offer some defence from flies and midges.

Shearing generally takes place in spring, as the fleece starts to lift. This helps to prevent overheating during warmer summer temperatures, and also makes it easier for lambs to feed.

Inspect sheep regularly, paying particular attention to the feet for evidence of disease, also the wool and skin, which can harbour parasitic infestations.

ALPACAS

Alpacas are environmentally friendly animals that are easy to keep and lovely to behold. Related to the llama, another herd animal, alpacas are naturally curious, docile and friendly creatures, and can be very affectionate when handled correctly. They make excellent companions for other animals, such as horses, sheep, goats, and even chickens. Alpaca fleece is incredibly soft and light, widely sought for its luxurious feel and durable quality. It is

BELOW: As herding animals, alpacas are only happy in a group; up to six can be kept on an acre of land.

OPPOSITE: Alpacas are charming animals, valued for their soft and luxurious fleece.

naturally hypoallergenic and much lighter, warmer and less itchy than sheeps' wool. The fibre is also popular for home spinning, or it can be sent to specialist processors to be turned into fabric or knitting yarn.

MAKING A CHOICE

Alpacas come in a wide range of colours – from white, fawns, browns and greys through to black and multi-coloureds. They communicate particularly through tail and ear positions and by making a range of curious humming sounds.

It is a good sign if an alpaca looks healthy and cared-for. But you will also want to check vaccination and worming records, and whether or not the animal is registered, in which case its parents and pedigree can be checked.

ACCOMMODATION

It is important to remember that alpacas are herd animals, and will live happier, healthier lives if they have the company of at least one other of their own kind, preferably two. Up to six alpacas can be kept on an acre of land, in which case hand-feeding at various times throughout the year may be required, depending on the quality of

the pasture. A pair of gelded males or a pair of females are ideal and are easily cared for by beginners.

FEEDING
Alpacas are hardy animals, and feeding with hay or alpaca pellets is only necessary if the pasture is thin or over-grazed; the animals are keen grazers and browsers and will tackle bark or leaves, so it is wise to fence off young shrubs or trees. It is important to have a source of water available to them at all times.

ABOVE: Have alpacas professionally sheared once a year, also taking the opportunity to get their toenails and teeth trimmed.

OPPOSITE: Correct feeding is important for good health and is reflected in the quality of the fleece.

Alpacas can be given a daily vitamin/mineral supplement, which also helps with training, and pregnant females and youngsters should also have extra protein feeds. Extra hay can be given in winter.

HEALTH

Alpacas like plenty of attention but minimal care to keep them healthy and happy, and they are normally vaccinated and wormed twice a year. Their toenails are trimmed two or three times a year, and their four large front teeth may need trimming once a year, which is easiest done when the shearer comes to call.

Diet and nutrition have a bearing on the fineness and density of an alpaca's fleece, and animals that are overfed will produce fleeces with a higher (coarser) micron count than those on a properly balanced diet. Drastic changes of diet, or high levels of stress. will directly affect the quality of the fibre produced by the animal at that time.

INDEX

ACKNOWLEDGEMENTS

Front Cover: Top left: ©istockphoto/Michael Westhoff. Top centre: ©istockphoto/ Carole Gomez. Top right: Flickr/Creative Commons: WXMom. Below left: Flickr/Creative Commons: Keven Law. Below centre: Flickr/Creative Commons: Maessive/Nico. Below right: Flickr/Creative Commons: SearchNET Media. Back Cover: Flickr/Creative Commons: Tyler Conklin. Spine: Flickr/Creative Commons: redjar.

The following photographs were supplied through © istockphoto, courtesey of the following photographers: Aaron Holbrough: page 218. Andsem: page 210 below. Annedde: page 151. AtWaG: page 213. Catnap72: pages 147, 156, 174. Christian Carroll: page 202 left. Dan Moore: page 196 left. Darla Hallmark: pages 146, 155. Derek Thomas: page 148. Doug Schneider: page 165. Dusan Zidar: page 192. Edward Ralph: page 201. Eric Delmar: page 166. Gustavo Andrade: page 191. Heinz Waldukat: page 143 above. Iain Sargeant: pages 201 above, 209 above. James Whittaker: pages 150, 161. Javier Robles: page 172. Johnyscriv: page 208. Jörg Kaschper: page 143 below. Jose Juan Garcia: page 154. June Lloyd: page 153. Kenneth Wiedermann: page 164 left. Kkgas: page 153. Kristian Septimus Krogh: page 164 right. Lawrence Sawyer: page 216. Linda Alstead: page 210 above. Liv Friis-Larsen: page 193 left. Lloyd Paulson: page 177. Magdelena Kucova: page 193. Malerapso: page 211. Mark Rasmussen: page 200 left. Martin Macarthy: page 171. Michael Westhoff: page 142 below. Monika Adamcyk: page 194. Noam Armonn: pages 175, 199. PeJo29: page 197. Peter Engelsted Jonasen: page 163. Phil Berry: page 180. Proximinder: pages 181, 185, 186. Rachel Giles: page 169. Ramon Rodriguez: pages 199 left, 217. Rebecca Picard: page 195. Ruchos: page 209 below. Sergiy Goruppa: page 145. Simon Smith: page 159. Suernat: pages 6-7. Tomasz Szymanski: page 190 right. Tony Campbell: page 221.

The following photographs were supplied through Flickr/Creative Commons www.creativecommons.org courtesy of the following photographers: Alan Levine: page 28 above. Allan Hack: page 205. Alexandre Dulaunoy: pages 8 above, 72 above. Alh1: pages 36, 39. AmandaLeighPanda: page 60. Amanda Slater: pages 91 below, 230. Andrea de Poda: page 198. Andrey: page 99. Andy Carter: page 37. Andy Wright: page 48. Angavelen in Veelinge: pages 223, 224 left, 225. Aunt jo jo: page 182. Aunt Owwee: page 126. Aussiegal: page 115. Bellybe_Khe: page 222 above. Bong Grit: pages 222 left, 244. Braphie: page 84 left. Brian Kelly: page 212. Bulaclac Paruparu: page 204 below. Caitlin Childs: page 56. Care_SMC: page 72 left. Cheekycrows3: page 127. Chris Morriss: page 227 above. Chris Gladis: page 128.Clarity: page 239. Clayirvine: pages 52 left, 90 right. Clayton O'Neill: page 63 left. Clotho98: page 106. Colin Howley: page 183. Crystal: page 92 left. Damien Cugley: page 35 below. Dan Meineck: page 58 left. Darren Copley: page 25. Daryl_Michell: page 84 left. Dawin Bell: pages 42, 88 right. Dawn Endico: page 79. D70focus: pages 162, 168, 190 left, 190 left. Dean (lew): page 226. Dichohecho: page 65 left. Don LaVange: page 121. Doviende/Pete: page 47. Dsa66503: page 41. Duchamp: page 246. Ed Yourdon: page 85. Elliott Brown: page: 26. Emma Jane Hogbin: page 96 left. Eric Hoffman: page 122. Ernesto Andrade: page 51 left. Fishermansdaughter: pages 52 right, 152, 158, 167, 188, 189.FotoosVanRobin: pages 76, 109. Geishaboy500: page 97. Gemma Longman: pages 33, 34 left. G-Kat2: page 80. Gilgongo: page 45 right. Gill Clardy. Glen Bowman: page 118. Gordon Joly: pages 14 below, 89 below. GT6JIM: page 233. Hans Splinter: pages 214, 243. Heather Hopkins: page 237. Holly Rowland: page 20. Ian Sutton: page 144. ILoveButter: pages 5, 228 left, 229. ...jc.... : page 22. Jeff Kubina: pages 101, 110, 248. Jenniferwoods: page 88 left. Jeremy Keith: pages 44 left, 57, 120. Jhm54/Jim: page 203. Joe de Luca: page 170. Johnathan Nightingale: page 81 above. John Haslam: page 105. Johnnyalive: page 27 Jolien_vallens: page 45 left. Karol M: page 64. Kevin Law: page 232. Kieran Jonnalagadda: page 117. Larry Page: page: 66 left. Laurel Fan: page 111. Linda N: pages 43, 50, 58. Linux Librarian: page 252. Living in Monrovia: page 30. Liz West: pages 59, 69, 70 both, 75 left, 91 above, 107, 116, 251. Maessive/Nico: page 234 right. Manjith Kainickara: pages 14 top, 87. Mark Robinson: page 227 below. Mark Shirley: page 19. Martin Pettitt: page 224 right. Matt Buck: page 38. Matt McGee: page 119 both. Matt Steppings: page 215. Megan Fizell: page 78 right. Michael Derr: page 18. Michael Wade: page 253. Miika Silfverberg: pages 100 right, 108. Mitch Lorens: page 82. Mrs Gemstone: page 125. Mtsn: page 46 left. Muppet: page 200 right. Mwri: page 102 right. Naitokz: page 94. net_efekt: pages 4, 16, 21, 40, 51, 53, 89 above. Nick McPhee: pages 32 left, 34 right, 35 above right. Norwichnuts:page 95 left. OakleyOriginals: page 66 right. Oli Bac: page 129. OohCaffiene: page 142 above. Patrick Breen: page 31. Paul Albertella: pages 35 above left, 102 left. Paul Joseph: page 75 right. Peter Birkinshaw: page 46 right. Peter Mulligan: page 245. PinAdd: page 81 below. PiX1066: page 93 below. Pizzodisevo: page 44 right. P. Markham: pages 3, 235, 240, 241 right. Pollinator: page 187 right. Quinn Dombrowski: pages 2, 55, 96 right. Rachel Black: page 149. Randen Pederson: page 228 right. Rasmus Lerdorf: pages 114 below, 123. Redjar: page 9. Rich Stylinski: page 62. Righolmer: page 29. Rob & Stephanie Levy: page 204 above. Robyn Gallagher: page 65 below. Rumble1973: pages 13 right, 176. Russell Yarwood: page 71. Rusty-grass: pages 67, 92 right. Sandy Austin: page 83. See-ming Lee: page 74. Sgustin78: page 17.Simon Blackley: page 103. S72/Jackie: page 247. Sky_Mitch: page 114 above. Sleepyneko/Eunice: pages 54, 73.Sling@Flickr: page 63 right. SlinZero: page 23. SnapsterMax: page 10. Snickclunk: page 68 right. Stereograb: page 97. Steve Jurvetson: page 238. Steve Maw: page 68left. Sygnus921: page 77. Tambako the Jaguar: pages 98 above, 112, 120, 234 left.Tasty bit: page 184. Terren in Virginia: page 86. Thomas Kreise: page 100 left. The bottom-moog: page 15. The Marmot: pages 32 right, 78 left. Till Westermayer: page 49. Treehouse1977: pages 104, 249. Twicepix: page 222 below right, 231. Tyler Conklin: page 250. Versageek: page 98 below. Wohach: page 178 Woodleywonderworks: page 206. World Resources Institute Staff: page 90 left. WXMom: page 113. Ydhsu/Daniel: page 61.Ynskjen: page 241 left. Yoppy: page 93 above. Zero1: page 11.

The following photographs have been supplied through Wikimedia Commons courtesy of the following photographers: Eigene Autnahme: page 173 below. Petr Wilgus: page 8 below. Robert Engelhardt: page 157, 160 below, 187 left.'Waugsberg: page: 179.